Two Autobiographical Plays

This volume contains two recently performed plays by John Arden, one a radio play, the other a short stage play. Both are strongly personal in flavour: each text is in its way indispensable for a proper understanding of Arden's dramatic art.

The Bagman or *The Impromptu of Muswell Hill*, a ninety-minute radio play, was first broadcast in 1970, directed by Martin Esslin. *The True History of Squire Jonathan and his Unfortunate Treasure* is a haunting ballad-like play about a miserly mediaeval squire: written some years ago, it was first staged at the Ambiance Lunch-Hour Theatre Club in 1968.

The photograph of John Arden on the back of the cover is reproduced by courtesy of Roger Mayne.

plays by John Arden

★

SERJEANT MUSGRAVE'S DANCE
THE WATERS OF BABYLON
LIVE LIKE PIGS
THE HAPPY HAVEN
THE WORKHOUSE DONKEY
IRONHAND (adapted from Goethe's *Goetz von Berlichingen*)
LEFT-HANDED LIBERTY
ARMSTRONG'S LAST GOODNIGHT
SOLDIER, SOLDIER AND OTHER PLAYS

plays by John Arden and Margaretta D'Arcy

★

THE BUSINESS OF GOOD GOVERNMENT
THE ROYAL PARDON
THE HERO RISES UP

Two Autobiographical Plays

The True History of Squire Jonathan and his Unfortunate Treasure

and

The Bagman or *The Impromptu of Muswell Hill*

by
JOHN ARDEN

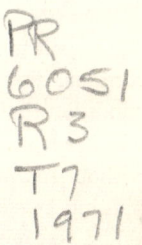

METHUEN & CO. LTD
11 NEW FETTER LANE · LONDON EC4

This edition first published in 1971
by Methuen and Co. Ltd
Squire Jonathan and His Unfortunate Treasure
© 1968 by John Arden
The Bagman or *The Impromptu of Muswell Hill*
Copyright © 1971 by John Arden
Printed in Great Britain by
Cox & Wyman Ltd Fakenham, Norfolk

SBN 416 09040 0 Hardback
SBN 416 09230 6 Paperback

All rights whatsoever in this play are strictly reserved and application for performance etc., should be made to Margaret Ramsay Ltd, 14a Goodwin's Court, London WC2. No performance may be given unless a licence has been obtained.

This book is available in hardbound and paperback editions. The paperback edition is sold subject to the condition that it shall not, by way of trade or otherwise, be lent, resold, hired out, or otherwise circulated without the publisher's prior consent in any form of binding or cover other than that in which it is published and without a similar condition including this condition being imposed on the subsequent purchaser.

to RUDI DUTSCHKE:

'I think, therefore I am',
Descartes, in prison, said.
Surrounded by stone walls
He was alone with his own head.

Rudi, being free
In a mobile free society,
Had a wound in *his* head:
But he was not alone:
His walls were made of paper
Not of stone.

He thinks, therefore they followed him about.
He thinks, therefore he scarcely dared go out.
He thinks, therefore they damn well threw him out.

Contents

AUTHOR'S PREFACE 9

The True History of Squire Jonathan
and his Unfortunate Treasure
19

The Bagman *or*
The Impromptu of Muswell Hill
35

Author's Preface

A SECOND DEDICATION

I dedicate these two plays printed here
To all those nosey-parkers who prefer
To know the poet's life and what he does
Rather than read his words upon the page
Or listen to them spoken on the stage.
Where and with whom he sleeps, and whom he meets –
Bending his knees or turning out his toes –
And what he cooks and how he sits and eats
Is far more interesting to us all
Than any tired old tale he wants to tell.
(Moreover, if the fellow goes and writes a play
You can't get in to see it unless you pay.)

I specially desire this dedication
To warm the hearts of those whose cold devotion
In setting down the facts and piling archives
Within an air-conditioned Institute
Produces, for themselves, a Doctorate:
And for the poet, death – while he still lives.

I also wish my small voice to be heard
By one particular zealous officer
From the Special Branch of Scotland Yard –
He'll know it, if he reads it, he wears a beard
And questioned me for nearly half-an-hour*
In 1969 at the platform-gate
That leads to the Irish boat at Holyhead.

---

* I think, because I too wore a beard,
  I was an Agitator, therefore to be feared.
  His own beard, no doubt, was a cute disguise –
  He had to watch for dangerous Irishmen:
  A growth of hair upon the chin
  In such wild company is not unwise.

When I came off the train he lay in wait
And asked me who I was and what I did.
I said
My name was Arden and I was a writer –
His gloomy face did not become much brighter.
Indeed I was most closely interrogated:
What were my politics, for whom had I voted,
Had I ever been arrested, had I ever been convicted?
He made me tell the story of my life.
But, strange, he asked no questions about my wife –
And she is Irish and most radical –
I thought he would have asked, for she might well
Keep guns along with love wrapped up in bed . . .
He let me go at last, he shook his head,
He was not satisfied . . . Now he may read
These two short plays Methuen has printed here:
He will discover what he has to fear.

Here I tell all and I hold nothing back:
I stand and wait for the counter-attack.

A Few Historical Facts

(relating to the background of the plays):

Facts about 'Squire Jonathan': About eighteen years ago I was in love with a large blonde beautiful Scot. I told her I wrote plays and poems and such-like. I shewed her a sample or two. She said: 'Oh dear . . . you really mean all this, don't you?' After some length of time I asked her if she would marry me. She said not. I protested that our acquaintance had been of sufficient duration and intimacy as to require her to give reason for her refusal. She said: 'Because you are a poet.' I said I thought that that was not a good reason and that furthermore much of my recent verse had been written in celebration of herself, and she had expressed herself pleased with it. She said that made it worse. Then, as we were stepping into an electric train, a rude man of about sixty pushed out past us, muttering curses under his breath. He had grey hair, becoming bald, a tight ill-tempered mouth, a pair of horn-rimmed spectacles, a briefcase and a black umbrella. He had perhaps had a bad day at the office. I said: 'I suppose you want me to secure a steady job in my regular profession (architecture), and end up like him?' She said: 'But that's how you are going to end up anyway.' Then she gave a gasp of alarm and her eyes went wide: 'Oh my goodness, I really think you *are*!' ... After that evening there was less of an intimacy between us: and eventually, without telling me what she was up to, she took herself off and married a character in the antique trade – a Turk, was he? Or a Syrian? – who was reputed to have been at one time a smuggler, and who was at least twice my age. I only ever caught one glimpse of him: under artificial light in a coffee bar – he looked like Jack Palance – oh yes, indeed *sinister*, but had Orpheus been able to flash that sort of smile he would have needed no harp to haul Eurydice out of hell. My displacement in his favour occurred at the end of 1956. By 1963, when I wrote the play, I no longer bore anybody any malice.

Facts about 'The Bagman': This play is in the nature of a dream. Some people think dreams foretell the future. This one in certain respects did. I wrote it in the spring of 1969. Later in the same year I became awkwardly involved with a group of revolutionists, one of whom, a lodger in my house, was arrested for throwing a petrol-bomb at a policeman during a demonstration in front of Ulster House, London. The people of the Bogside, Derry, were at that time beleaguered by an extraordinary body of seventeenth-century Calvinists, wearing uniform, armed with CS gas, and laughably entitled 'The Forces of Law-and-Order'. The Bogsiders repelled their advances with petrol-bombs: the one thrown in front of Ulster House was intended as a reminder to the London Fs of L & O that the Irish Catholics of the Six Counties had a number of friends elsewhere. The boy who threw it deduced correctly that the seventeenth-century Calvinists would not have been so bold if various groups of rich twentieth-century Agnostics on this side of the water had extracted no advantage from their goings-on. It is not only a question of extracting advantage, of course – it's a matter of active encouragement of sectarian strife in order to secure a docile disunited labour-force in Northern Ireland – James Connolly had it taped sixty years ago, but it seems an impossible task to make the British public ever understand that the 'Irish problem' has always been a 'British problem' and nothing else. The Protestants were *put* into Ireland in the reign of James I for the purpose of consolidating the royal power there, and also for the purpose of making certain Britons rich. It still goes on. My lodger wanted to bring, as it were, the battle back home, to the place from which it receives its continual occult direction. His strategy was sound: but I was unable to approve the particular tactic he chose to implement it.

The bomb had hit nothing – neither man nor building – a policeman had beaten the flames out in a second with a placard snatched from a lounging demonstrator. But even had a constable been burnt to death the cause would not have been advanced. Indeed, such a holocaust would only have confirmed the British public in their habitual blind assumption that all Irishmen (and their friends) are frantic drunken ruffians to whom arson is as mother's milk. All this was debated in my house, day and night, between his remand on bail and his eventual trial.* (He was sent to prison for several months, which surprised no one.) I do not think I need go into those interminable debates in detail: except to say that I was described – in a hostile spirit – as a 'Bourgeois Liberal'. I don't know that this was correct – to my way of thinking a 'Bourgeois Liberal' is a man who would have offered his patronizing solidarity to the comrades, while, at the same time, deploring *on principle* their use of *violence*. Although I was the Honorary Chairman of *Peace News*, I did not raise any such principled objection. The residents of the Bogside had had little choice but to be violent, and the sight of their battle on the television had 'stirred my heart as with a trumpet'. My feelings towards the capitalist/unionist/protestant Junta in the Six Counties were – and still are – very violent. But I did feel that this particular bomb had been

---

* I should point out, by the by, that his bomb business took place some months *after* the incident at Holyhead Station described in the verses above. If it had happened before, there might just possibly have been a bit of rhyme or reason to the detective's questions.

thrown at the wrong time and the wrong target – or rather, at a confused target: was it Ulster House (OK, perhaps); a policeman (why? In contrast to his Derry colleagues, he was unarmed); or, generally, the entire gathering (dreadful!)? – and above all, it had been thrown ineffectively. Further, the young man was trying to maintain a plea of 'not guilty' – he defied the police to prove he had thrown anything. This sort of defence, though permissible in most court cases, seemed oddly unsuitable in the context, and would have deprived him of the opportunity of explaining his action forcefully from the dock. He was, I thought, badly in need of such an opportunity, in view of the type of publicity the bomb had already had in the newspapers.

Of course, I realize that he – and his friends – were angry with me for reasons that had little to do with theoretical ideology. He had the historic distaste of the warrior for the man of words. He had, after all, put himself at risk in a battle – even if the battle had been rather unilateral and not of proven necessity – and I had not. I had been Sitting On The Fence. Under such circumstances, it is no good trying to argue that the only place a writer *can* usefully be is On The Fence, or else how will he be able to see what is going on clearly enough to write about it afterwards? That argument is anyway based on a pretty shifty half-truth. I have no doubt that choleric Norman barons used to bellow at their *jongleurs*: 'Where were *you* in 1066, you Pacifist Idealist, you!' To which, if the *jongleur* was an honest man, the answer would probably have been: 'Hiding in a tent at the back of the camp, scared to death...'

It may perhaps be wondered how, if I was Honorary Chairman of *Peace News*, I did *not* adopt a principled attitude of non-violence towards the Ulster House Outrage. But just about at that time I resigned from the Honorary Chair. The reason I gave to the Board was that I was about to travel overseas and did not wish to hold such a post when it was not possible for me to attend the monthly meetings. There was another reason, however, which I did not give to the Board, because I did not really give it to myself until a good deal later. A prestige position on a pacifist newspaper was, I came to feel, at any rate for myself, a classic piece of Fence-Sitting. It enabled me to offer pronouncements upon public affairs from a position of safety – I could attack governments and Fs of L & O with enthusiasm, while at the same time avoiding direct action and its consequent peril for myself by pleading my principles. *Non*-violent direct action – often more dangerous than the violent variety – I did not take part in, much, because I was not persuaded of its value at the present time. So altogether I discovered myself in a sufficiently dishonest attitude. So I quit.

I then went to India. In India the war between the fed men and the hungry men, the clothed men and the naked men, the sheltered men and the exposed men, is being waged with great ferocity, compared to which the manifestation outside Ulster House had the appearance of one of those fifteenth-century tourneys where the knights were so heavily armed that they could scarcely ever be seriously hurt, where a wooden barrier between contestants protected even the horses from collision, and where all contestants were of the same social class. (By Indian standards *everyone* in England is of the same social class. The Western proletariat is the oppressive bourgeoisie of the East – the class struggle is now being waged across continental divides instead of 'across the tracks' in one country at a time. To an Indian revolutionist there is no such thing as a Left-wing Western writer. If he is Western he is – by definition – an agent of the Right.)

While in India I had some opportunity to see the non-violence of the late Mahatma Gandhi in action. It did not impress me much. There is also in India a violent movement of Marxist–Leninist derivation known as the Naxalite movement. This includes university intellectuals from the cities and also landless peasants from up-country. I was not, of course, able to meet any of the latter. Even if I had known how to speak their language, or they mine, the very fact of their having conversed with a foreigner would have rendered them under suspicion from the local Fs of L & O. (As usual the authorities there are only too eager to blame all disturbances upon the ubiquitous Outside Agitator.) But I did talk with a few of the university revolutionist element in Delhi and Calcutta. It appeared that they – in contrast with all previous radical movements in India – were making their appeal to the really hungry, naked, exposed men of the sub-continent, the low-caste, out-caste, and often aboriginal peasants – men who had no lands of their own, and who were burdened from their very conception with debts owed to landlords which they could not hope to pay off in their own lifetime, and which therefore condemned them to a servitude such as we have not seen in England since the collapse of the mediaeval feudal system. The Gandhian non-violent workers had for several years been begging the land-owners to give some small proportion of their acreage for the use of the landless masses: but their well-meaning sermons had received little response. Gifts of land had been promised, but the promises had not been kept – or, if kept, the land had turned out to be barren and useless unless much money was to be spent upon irrigation, and who was to provide the money? But now, the growth of Naxalite activity had given the Gandhians a new argument. 'If you will not make over your lands to the poor,' they would say, 'the Naxalites will kill you. You had better listen to us before it is too late.' I did not find this approach particularly high-principled. The Naxalite guerrillas were being used, as it were, as the violent arm of the non-violent movement. And they are indeed a violent arm. They carry out selective murders of landlords and money-lenders, whose severed heads they leave exposed on posts outside their villages. This bloodshed is less cowardly and underhand than it seems. The men they kill are protected by a venal caste-conscious police as well as by private squads of ugly thugs, who will cheerfully burn a peasant's house and all his family if he is so bold as to ask for more than he is already permitted to have. 'Murder' is the wrong word – the Naxalites say 'Execution' or 'An act of war'. I agree with them.

I was unfortunate enough to run up against the Fs of L & O in India. And as a result I spent a few days in the Shillong District Jail. It was a very minor incident, really – the absence of a Foreigner's Permit for the restricted area of Assam: an offence which anyone could commit – so incompetent were the arrangements made by the Government in apprising foreigners of their need to obtain this document – and which does not normally carry with it any worse penalty than expulsion from the area, together with an illegible endorsement on one's passport. But I – or rather, my companion and I – for I rarely stick my neck out unless goaded to it by someone for whose opinion I have respect – had not been too compliant with the police. Questions had been asked about warrants and authority: this had not been liked: it meant – to an Indian policeman, at any rate – that I was a person of 'obvious Communist bent'. (I *am*, now.) So, in order to teach us a lesson, we were slung inside to await trial: instead of being allowed to handle the whole thing over the desk of some courteous official, drinking his tea and puffing at his cigarettes. My belongings were searched and I was found to be in possession of sundry *books* of an 'anti-state nature'. I hadn't written any of these myself, alas. But the dangerous potentialities of literature were, for the first time in my life at first hand, made clear to me. In a country where possession of the works of Mao and Lenin – though this is not exactly *forbidden* – can get a man into prison for an unspecified length of time, the writer begins to take a more encouraging view of the value of his craft than he can normally do in Britain. Also, while I was held in the jail, I had conversation with the other prisoners in my ward. Most of them were there for 'political' reasons. They were awaiting trial like me, but, unlike me, they had no reason to believe that they would ever be brought to court. Some of them had been there for three years. Perhaps one day, when the government decides they are no longer a danger, they will be quietly released. Perhaps that day will never come. They were, in many cases, men of education and wide reading. I talked to them about the Relationship of the Writer to his Public in Times of Social Upheaval: and this typical Western seminar-subject took on an altogether different appearance than it could possibly do in London or even Chicago.

It will be obvious that if I had written *The Bagman* after, instead of before, the events I have here outlined, the play would not have turned out at all in the same way. I considered rewriting the last part of it but I decided against this, because it does reflect fairly enough the state of my mind in the spring of 1969: and I thought it would be better to demonstrate my opinions of 1971 in a new play – which is not yet written. But I should note, for the benefit of the reader, that the attitude of the central character at the end of the story is reprehensible, cowardly, and not to be imitated. The play has, I believe, been praised by some critics apparently on the ground that it deals with an 'Important Modern Dilemma' common to all artists, and so on.... Our critics love to be able to write things like that. It gives them a sense of warm communion with the artist. 'After all,' they muse, 'if Poet X and Playwright Y can't sort out their own integrity, why should I worry about mine? Did not the Emperor Nero believe that, were the truth only told, he would be found to be no more perverted than anyone else? These works of art shew that their creators are as cowardly and as time-serving as I am. So I can continue, without qualms, to write my hack-column for this terrible old press-lord – whom, of course, I would cheerfully assassinate if I could...' I am not flattered by such persons. Mao Tsetung, that succinct poet, has said, 'Whatever the enemy opposes, we must support: whatever the enemy supports, we must oppose.' Or words to that effect. I hope I have made clear in *The Bagman* (for otherwise I would not have wished it to be published) that I recognize as the enemy the fed man, the clothed man, the sheltered man, whose food, clothes, and house are obtained at the expense of the hunger, the nakedness, and the exposure of so many millions of others: and who will allow anything to be *said*, in books or on the stage, so long as the food, clothes, and house remain undiminished in his possession.

John Arden (1971)

The True History
of Squire Jonathan
and his Unfortunate Treasure

The True History of Squire Jonathan and his Unfortunate Treasure was first performed by the Ambiance Lunch-Hour Theatre Club on June 17 1968, with the following cast:

SQUIRE JONATHAN	Ian Trigger
A BLONDE WOMAN	Jenny Lee
DARK MEN	Richard Stuart
	Bernard Boston

Directed by Ed Berman

The scene is set in wild country several centuries ago.

The interior of a stone tower. One low round-arched door, and a little window with a deep embrasure. A minimum of furniture: but one prominent iron-bound wooden chest. The style of the décor and costumes is what one might call 'Grimm fairy-tale Gothic'. JONATHAN *squats alone in the tower – he is dressed in clothes which have once been quite splendid but are now soiled, threadbare and patched. The room is lit by the glow of a great fire of logs.*

JONATHAN. I am a small man and nothing about me is large. Look at me. My features are small, confined and tight. My hair is red – an unbecoming red – I do not want to hear anybody say it is the colour of the hair of Judas. My teeth are good, hard, yellow, not large, but sharp – as sharp and as dangerous as those of an unreliable dog. When provoked I can bring them together very suddenly indeed and very cruelly. I have in my time taken bites out of the backs of ankles. Malignant ankles. And I am prepared to do so again if my personal convenience is threatened. If I were to remove my clothes – if I were to remove them (which I do not intend to do) – yet – if I were – I say – to remove my clothes, you would be confronted with a body as cadaverous as it is hairy, with ribs like prongs of a garden fork, a navel like an egg-cup full of dust, a ridiculously wrinkled pair of cullions, and a well-loved drooping yard that very badly desires employment. Employment other than that afforded it periodically by my own unsatisfied fingers. I also have flat feet. The total aspect of my person would in fact be absurd and unlikely to give pleasure to any woman save for the most depraved: unless she were able, by the intensity of her spirit, to peer right through the flesh of this rotten carcass and to discern within it the intensity of *my* spirit, my small spirit, a bluebottle fly whirring and gyrating in the prison of a glass jar. That is how I am, myself within myself, and here is how I am, myself within this tower – here I live alone. I am descended from kings. These stones were erected in ancient days, by such kings, for the fortifications of their glory, and the pleasure of their pride. I had in mind once to decorate my tower, to wash its walls with snow-white lime and to prick them out with rectilinear patterns of gold, of blue, and of scarlet. I had in mind also to rear several pinnacles striped like a barber's pole, and to hang therefrom clanging banners of beaten copper and vanes of gilded zinc to revolve in the run of the west wind and delight my eyes by their rotation and my ears by their twittering music. All this I have failed to achieve. However. However . . . I have been compensated. Here is a large black box.

> Within this box
> Controlled by bolts and locks,
> Not yet available to you
> But known alone to me,
> Lives in its quiet life my true
> Inherited treasure, and my love.
> You shall see.
> Here is the dream that makes my small heart move.

He opens the chest. It is full of treasure, which he shows in handfuls to the audience.

Gold. Basically gold. There are also articles of silver, platinum and various other semi-precious metals. Chrys-elephantine work (that is, carved ivory with a golden inlay), enamel work from Limoges, engraved cameos of sardonyx, beryl, malachite and so forth. A great quantity of jewels, cut and uncut, with and without appropriate settings, you see there are brooches, chains, earrings, belts, bangles, finger-rings, toe-rings, nostril-rings, as well as tiaras, crowns, coronets, carcanets, epaulettes and elaborately worked buttons. Also latchets for shoes and fastenings for garters. Here is a necklace. Here is another. Pearls, diamonds, rubies. Emeralds. Emeralds are green. Green as the eyes of a great blonde milky woman. A giantess. A mountain. A green mountain with the warmth of the sunshine turning the clouds about its head to gold. Gold at the top of the mountain. Gold and white silver in the bottom of my box. For fifteen years I have waited for my mountain of a white woman. I have looked out at my small window and watched for her to come to me. Without such a woman all this treasure is worthless. For fifteen years I saw nobody, except the swearing cowherds in their brown coats squelching through the ruts behind their foul-arsed bullocks – and occasionally – across the bog – one or two of the Dark Men who walked deviously with long sticks. Dark Men, in broad tattered hats and wrapped up in tatters against the damp air, they walk with a curious stiffness as though upon stilts – and I know where they come from. They come from the forest at the other side of the bog, and they come around me to spy. They know about my treasure. Or, if they don't know, they suspect it. But my walls are too strong, and they walk around and look up at them from under their broken hat-brims and they sing their filthy jeering songs at me, and then they go back to their uncomfortable camp-fires and burn some more of their damned charcoal (for such is their trade in the forest) and they lay some more plots and they send out more spies – next week will it be – or most certainly next month – for I tell you they are at it always . . . Listen, do you hear them? Filthy jeering songs. Listen to them. Listen!

DARK MEN (*singing, outside*).
>Johnny Johnny Johnny boy
>We know you're there
>Johnny Johnny Johnny gae and cut your hair:
>Cut your hair, boy,
>Cut your toes,
>Cut your nostrils oot o' your nose –

FIRST DARK MAN. If you're no gaun tae cut them yersel, Johnny, we can come in there and cut them for ye!

SECOND DARK MAN. We've got knives, Johnny, and strong forks.

FIRST DARK MAN. We've got oor spoons tae eat your porridge, Johnny!

They all laugh.

DARK MEN. Hey Johnny Johnny Johnny –
FIRST DARK MAN. Toss us oot a bit o' siller!
SECOND DARK MAN. Toss us oot a gowden cup to drink your health in –
FIRST DARK MAN. Or what about an auld tin jerrycan, Johnny, wi' glintin' diamonds on the handles?
SECOND DARK MAN. What about your piss-pot?
FIRST DARK MAN. What about the wee thin skull frae the top o' your neck-bane, Johnny?
SECOND DARK MAN. What about it, Johnny?
FIRST DARK MAN. What?
SECOND DARK MAN. What?
DARK MEN. What?

They all laugh.

FIRST DARK MAN. Johnny: we'll be back!

Their laughter recedes into the distance.

JONATHAN. But my walls are too strong for them. They have no weapons but their hatchets: how can such men as these expect to control artillery? And to reach inside of me – to reach deep in to my very mortal core – nothing short of carronades or howitzers can conceivably serve. And handled, moreover, by none but the most experienced of gunlayers ... Ah yes, you may come back – many times you may come back – but nothing for you, nothing for you, nothing, nothing – nothing!

He is looking out of the window, shouting after them: suddenly he breaks off, rubs his eyes, and looks again.

Aha – aha – no ... it is a very misty morning, I am deceived by the vapours, I must be hallucinated by the exhalation from the bog – no – no – I am not deceived neither – I can see what I can see. At last, at last, by the mercy of God (God's mercy and the good grace of the Holy Apostles, all twelve of them, twelve) after fifteen years at last – look – I can see her coming! My woman. On horseback ... Oh, I wonder what her name is? She has a grey horse, and an orange-tawny cloak upon her back, and under the cloak a gown of the brilliant green, and she rides around my inherited property on the other side of the drainage canal ... if the horse took fright, she might fall off ... I wonder what might make it take fright? ... If somebody were to make a rude noise – as it were –

He makes a rude noise.

– or louder perhaps –

He does it again.

– then she might fall off. Oh dear, she has fallen ... I wonder how that happened? Unexpected. Unfortunate ... Ah, the horse has run away. She's all covered with mud – what an enormous beautiful woman – huge – golden – green ...

BLONDE WOMAN (*calls from outside*). Hello –? I've had an accident. Can you let me in?

JONATHAN (*at the window*). Not in here. No.

BLONDE WOMAN. Please let me in.

JONATHAN steps down from the window.

JONATHAN (*to himself*). Oh, my my goodness me – no. That wouldn't do at all.

BLONDE WOMAN (*still outside*). Please.

JONATHAN. For suppose she were to prove avaricious, or even larcenous – and lay hands upon my treasure . . .

BLONDE WOMAN (*outside*). Please.

JONATHAN closes his box and pushes it away.

JONATHAN. No, of course not, I can't let her – no, it wouldn't do at all . . .

He opens the door and the BLONDE WOMAN *comes in.*

JONATHAN. Madam, do pray enter – accept my hospitality, so poor as it may seem, until you are quite recovered and repaired from the effects of your sad accident . . . yes, I witnessed it from the window, so untoward, so very startling, how could it have occurred? I fear there are malignant persons in this region who would not hesitate to cause distress to a lonely traveller for no better reason than the satisfaction of their own mischief . . . Madam, an unworthy chair – I beg you to be seated. Are you sure you are not hurt? Are you quite sure? Would you like to eat some breakfast? Or at least a cup of wine? Or – yes, there is some whisky – or the remains of my bottled beer – or perhaps a slice of toasted loaf? Sit down, please sit down. May I unfasten your mantle? It is a very heavy mantle, you must be very hot in it, despite the damp and the chill that pervade our dreary marshes. This brooch across your throat is of somewhat pedestrian design –

BLONDE WOMAN. Oh yes, I am afraid it is – had I known you were a connoisseur I would have chosen another one.

JONATHAN. Or would you be offended if I ventured to choose one for you?

He pulls out his box and opens it to take out a jewel.

JONATHAN. What about this? If you like it, it is yours. Do you like it? Do you?

BLONDE WOMAN. You are very kind.

JONATHAN. Look – I'll pin it in for you, then when you resume the mantle, it will provide an unparalleled fastening. There.

BLONDE WOMAN. Good sir, but you are too kind.

JONATHAN. I am looking at the comb in your hair.

BLONDE WOMAN. Tortoise-shell.

JONATHAN (*takes comb out of box*). Ivory. Here is one made of ivory. Let me put it in for you. Or rather, what I'll do is this: I'll fasten your hair, and then I'll put it in. An ivory comb, with a scene of Diana and Acteon carved upon it in relief – standing in the fountain and the water flowing over her . . . See, I'll put it here, and your hair can flow over also, to reinforce the effect of the water. You must not confine your hair. Far better to let it flow. Oh, heavy as the ebb tide – the ninth wave of the ebb tide –

BLONDE WOMAN. I've never had it cut.

JONATHAN. You must be very hot. I keep a large fire going because of the inclement vapours. I have already referred to them. You should take off your gown. Look – let me unfasten it for you . . . This belt you wear – unornamented leather. Would you not prefer a gold one?

BLONDE WOMAN. If I am taking the gown off, I shall not need one at all.

JONATHAN. No. No more you will . . .

Gown off.

You are wearing no necklace or earrings.

BLONDE WOMAN. I have very little money. My great-uncle

may die soon and leave me his fortune, but until such time as he does, I have nothing whatever. My father gives me nothing.

JONATHAN. What about your garters?

BLONDE WOMAN. Cotton.

JONATHAN. Constricting. Prevent the free flow of the blood. Agony. Varicose veins.

Garters off.

BLONDE WOMAN. You are very thoughtful.

JONATHAN. And your stockings are soaking wet where you fell on the wet grass.

Stockings off.

BLONDE WOMAN. You are thoughtful and kind ... I will not permit you to take off any more.

JONATHAN. Indeed not. Unless you wish me to.

BLONDE WOMAN. Not yet. Shall we say not yet?

JONATHAN. Put on this necklace. Or shall I put it on for you?

BLONDE WOMAN. Whatever you like. I am tired.

JONATHAN. Tired, damp, and indolent ... you are not unlike my marshes. And the earrings.

BLONDE WOMAN. If you must.

JONATHAN. No, this pair does not suit you. I thought maybe emeralds, but a contrast with the colour of your eyes now appears to me more striking. Here are rubies. Shall you wear them?

BLONDE WOMAN. I have truly no great preference. But you might offer me a mirror.

JONATHAN. Here you are. I apologize for the crack in it.

BLONDE WOMAN. Without a doubt the rubies are far better than the emeralds. Put them on for me. Thank you. You are so kind. You make me look beautiful.

JONATHAN. You must look beautiful all over. I do not approve the cut of this shift.

BLONDE WOMAN. It has no cut to speak of. That is its purpose. It is worn for warmth and decency.

JONATHAN. Ah – modesty . . .

BLONDE WOMAN. Unrevealing.

JONATHAN. Concealing.

BLONDE WOMAN. Not very good material.

JONATHAN. Cheap cotton stuff. Decent indeed: but not too warm, I should have thought.

BLONDE WOMAN. Linen. It is quite chilly.

JONATHAN. Linen of poor quality.

BLONDE WOMAN. Moreover, it is rather old. There are darns and patches in it. Look. I don't like it. Take it off.

Shift off.

Now, here I am. With what do you propose to cover me, instead?

JONATHAN. I am of the opinion that it would be better not to cover you. You have the earrings and the necklace, and the comb. What's this?

He indicates her chastity belt.

BLONDE WOMAN. It is locked. There is no key.

JONATHAN. How can there be no key?

BLONDE WOMAN. It was thrown away, for cruelty, into a deep pit full of rainwater and dead rotten branches.

JONATHAN. I dare say it could be broken.

BLONDE WOMAN. Do you think you have the strength? Your small hands are nervous: but they are not very strong. I am, as it were, chained. I would like some more chains. Golden chains.

JONATHAN. Solid gold.

BLONDE WOMAN. I think hung round my shoulders.

JONATHAN. I could put one around your waist.

BLONDE WOMAN. The belt would be better. You showed it to me earlier. Indeed and indeed you are exceedingly kind to me.

JONATHAN. I have circlets of little bells . . . Here we are . . . listen.

BLONDE WOMAN. You must put them around my ankles. You are nervous but very kind. You shall hear them, when I walk . . . Listen . . .

JONATHAN. Ah, you walk about my tower like a huge embellished elephant.

BLONDE WOMAN. Big enough, certainly.

JONATHAN. But smooth – and much whiter. They tell me the white elephants of the King of Siam are really a kind of blotchy grey.

BLONDE WOMAN. I am white and I am gold.

JONATHAN. You are chrys-elephantine. Carved out of gigantic ivory. Uncut hair all in my fingers – a great cap of beaten gold, chased and engraved, quite covering the quiet nape, and all down your back it falls, heavy, important, dominant, and then the small inlay, delicate, intricate, placed in your three places – here – here – and here – but where is it?

BLONDE WOMAN. Your hands are not strong enough. What about the emeralds?

JONATHAN. One: two.

BLONDE WOMAN. What about the rubies?

JONATHAN. One: two. Three: four. But these are not true rubies. It would be better to call them pearls. I will give you a golden garter.

BLONDE WOMAN. Why not a pair?

JONATHAN. Complete symmetry is not good. Indeed, I find it abhorrent. Ah, you have a rotten tooth at one side of your mouth.

BLONDE WOMAN. It doesn't hurt.

JONATHAN. I'm glad of that. Toothache is most terrifying – I have suffered from it myself only too often, all alone in this grim tower: I could not bear to imagine that you too had known such pain. But it improves your appearance.

BLONDE WOMAN. You do not mean that, surely?

JONATHAN. Why should I not mean it?

BLONDE WOMAN. I have always been ashamed of it and in order to hide it I have frequently distorted my lips. But I was afraid to have it pulled out. In my country they call the torturers in the King's Prisons the Royal Dentists. That is the sort of place I come from.

JONATHAN. No: I have already told you – it improves your appearance. I give you my word, you are *enhanced*. My name is Squire Jonathan: I am descended from Kings. If my forefathers' torturers were the same people as their dentists I am quite sure they would have been dismissed. But one black tooth among thirty-one that gleam so brilliantly is an object of great beauty in itself. Do not distort your lips: for your smile, as it is, is remarkable. Do you know, you smile so warmly?

BLONDE WOMAN. I smile so foolishly.

JONATHAN. Yes, I know: you're not intelligent. Warm you are, certainly, fat slow, with your passive movements – you great bolster, you lurching hay-cart, you vast unfolded circus-tent all a-flap and a-jingle in the buffet of the wind – but you don't use your brains. Now *I* never use anything else.

BLONDE WOMAN. Nothing else – whatever?

JONATHAN. I have no opportunity.

BLONDE WOMAN. Oh, I think you have now. Or if you were strong enough. Or could lay your hand upon a hacksaw.

JONATHAN. No. It is not necessary. It would be bound to be abortive . . . You have only come here to make me into a laughing-stock. You are waiting for the Dark Men.

BLONDE WOMAN. The Dark Men?

JONATHAN. You will wait until they come and call for you and then you will go off with them. You're just filling in the time here, that's all that you are doing! They will bring you back your horse and then you will ride off with them. When they take you to their forest there will be no jewels for you there, you know. They will not undress you there in a warm room with coloured cushions. But a miserable camp fire in the drizzling rain, where your body will be scorched or else it will be wet and cold – or maybe part-wet, part-scorched, burnt arse and frozen tits, and nothing for you to lie down in but the nettles and the black mud. I say no jewels for you there, you arrogant sneering strumpet – the best you can do there is to draw patterns on your skin like a cannibal savage with broken bits of their damned charcoal – for such is their nasty trade, you know. Charcoal burners. Animals. They will violate you among the nettles without offering you any adornment: and they will compel you to wash their abominable garments. Have you ever imagined the crusted filth and half-dried urine in the crutch of a charcoal-burner's trousers? Aha yes, I do disgust you! But I swear it is but a quarter of the disgust I feel for you! ... Where are you going?

BLONDE WOMAN. Away. You have become offensive. Three minutes ago you could have possessed my body: but instead you have tried to take possession of *me*: I am altogether too large for you.

She pulls off all the jewels, etc.

Here, put them back in your box. Comb, chains, garters, necklace, where is my mantle – give it to me –

JONATHAN. Don't take the brooch out of it –

BLONDE WOMAN. Your brooch, not mine. See, I will leave you the mantle with the pin still stuck into it. You can use it to pierce your ears to put in your own earrings – here they are – rubies –

JONATHAN. I shall give her to the Dark Men.
    They have teeth and they have axes:
    Let them cut her up and tear her.
    There is no woman I have ever seen
    With whom I would compare her.
    She is so huge and so white of her body
    She is above all the most selfish and vain lady

> I do not love her but I fear her:
> She is altogether too enormous.
> Let her go, let her go, to the dark charcoal-burners.

BLONDE WOMAN. I don't know who you are talking to, but if you are talking to me I will take you at your word. They are outside, are they not?

JONATHAN. Never mind where they are!

BLONDE WOMAN. Your brooch, not mine, but it still has its uses...

Chastity belt unpicked and taken off. JONATHAN *threatens her with a knife.*

BLONDE WOMAN. If you stab me with that blade you will find my cadaver far too heavy for you to lift. And then what will you do? Your situation is impossible. I will leave you to enjoy it.

She goes to the window.

> Where are the Dark Men? Where are you, you dirty wanderers? You disconnected fragments of uncoagulated soot – come and catch me – here I am!

DARK MEN (*outside*). Jump for it, lassie – we're here wi' a strang blanket – noo jump for it on the cry – wi' a yan, twa and a *three*!

She jumps out of the window.

> We caught her, we held her, my God, when she fell, what a roly-poly wobble – here's a meal for all the people! Johnny, we're right grateful, ye've fulfilled our wames this day!

FIRST DARK MAN. Ah Johnny, you're a grand wee man. Ye hae bestowed us what ye can!

SECOND DARK MAN. Ye're bauld and zealous
> Gay and generous,
> Here's a cheer frae a' the gang of us!

Their cheers, mixed with laughter, recede into the distance.

JONATHAN. And yet I am not defeated. She has left behind her every piece of my jewellery. Or has she? Where's the belt I put about her middle? Still about her. Still about her.
    It made creases in her flesh.
    It was scarcely to her advantage.
    She might as well keep it.
    I am not yet defeated.

The Bagman
or
The Impromptu of Muswell Hill

The Bagman or *The Impromptu of Muswell Hill* was first presented as a radio play on BBC Radio 3, on March 27 1970, with the following cast:

NARRATOR	Alan Dobie
OLD WOMAN	Hilda Kriseman
YOUNG WOMAN	Sheila Allen
POPULAR MINISTER	Geoffrey Matthews
UNPOPULAR MINISTER	Hector Ross
AMBASSADOR	Peter Pratt
KING	Austin Trevor
QUEEN	Margaret Wolfit
3 STARVING WOMEN	Hilda Kriseman
	Madi Hedd
	Sonia Fraser
OTHERS	Sean Barrett
	Wilfrid Carter
	John Rye
	David Spenser

Produced by Martin Esslin

Wind, rain, occasional traffic noises.

NARRATOR. Upon a Thursday afternoon, it being half-closing-day, I set out from my house along Muswell Hill Broadway in search of an evening newspaper. It was too early for the street-corner sellers to have set up their little placards, the newsagents were shut, and a wet north-west wind was scuttling between the houses.

> Upon the top of Muswell Hill
> I stood alone and felt quite ill
> Without the *Standard* or the *News*
> What could I do of any use?
> No word could I get of peace or war:
> So who was I, where was I,
> What was I for?
> If one had asked of me my name
> I freely could have told the same –
> John Arden (thirty-eight) of ancient family,
> Writer of plays for all the world to see,
> To see, and pay for, and to denigrate:
> Such was my work since 1958.
> I could not boast, like Cicero,
> That I had saved the state,
> Nor yet, like Catiline, that I had tried
> My fiercest best to have it all destroyed.
> If, on this soggy Thursday, I should fall down dead.
> What of my life and death would then be said?
> 'He covered sheets of paper with his babble,

He covered yards of stage-cloth with invented people,
He worked alone for years yet was not able
To chase one little rat from underneath the table.'
The rats would eat the cheese,
The cats would eat the rats,
In convenience and ease:
They would not notice any difference
For Arden's sudden disappearance.
There was no reason why they should.
So I walked alone to Highgate Wood.

Traffic noises recede.

Here in the cold park I wrapped my overcoat about me, sat down upon a bench, and tossed bread crumbs to the squirrels. The dead leaves blew between my feet and the stumps of the trees, the red buses at my back rumbled backwards and forwards out of sight upon the main road, and the children were all at school, so their play-ground was quite empty. As I sat there I fell asleep, and as I slept I dreamed a dream. Or rather it seemed that the dream rose up at me, from out of the rain-darkened sand-pit in the deserted children's playground, it piled itself up so very quickly, in a turbulence of sand and torn scraps of cigarette papers, it had something the shape of a dirty old woman, not quite in her right mind. She was asking me if I would buy from her some white heather or some clothes pegs ...

OLD WOMAN. White heather ...

NARRATOR. She was a nuisance there, I didn't want her ...

OLD WOMAN. Clothes pegs ...

NARRATOR. Go away, no no no – don't want anything ... thank you ...

OLD WOMAN. White heather brings good fortune –

NARRATOR. I've had good fortune, all too soon.

OLD WOMAN.
>And wooden pegs will hold it fast
>So that it will not fly away
>Peg down the luck you catch today
>And you will have it yet tomorrow.
>Peg down your joy, peg down your sorrow
>Examine them when you have time,
>Weigh the other against the one –
>You will not know what you can do
>Until you know what you have done.

NARRATOR. You're beginning to be tiresome, go, get you gone: Portentous oracular condemnatory old hag...

OLD WOMAN. I'll tell you what, how would you like
A beautiful useful canvas bag?
It's yours for ten shillings, with whatever it contains. It's pig-in-a-poke, in fact, all my young gentlemen take great delight to put at risk a few bob on a lucky-bag the like of this. Why, it's only last month I sold just such a one to a courageous lad from overseas, and he opened it up directly and what did he find –?

NARRATOR. Well, what did he find?

OLD WOMAN. He found such an elegant soft young woman, with golden skin like olive oil and black hair down to her sweet haunches as bright as melted bitumen. And she became his private property for evermore without regrets. What do you think to that, then?

NARRATOR. Most improbable.

OLD WOMAN. True.

NARRATOR.
>Whether true or false it was temptation:
>I was in a mood for fornication.
>And also I was, was I not, in a dream
>Where women are always exactly what they seem
>Instead of being no better than they are.
>In any case, I thought, I would not go too far:

> Open the bag, take just a quick peep,
> Put in my hand, make a tentative grope.
> If I did not like her I could quickly shove her back,
> Tie up the strings again round the mouth of the sack –
> For some fresh brief sexuality which might prove very nice
>
> Ten shillings did not seem to me an inordinate price.
> You don't mind a lot of small change?

Sound of money being counted.

OLD WOMAN. Oh no, sir, it's convenient really: there you are, sir, thank you . . .

NARRATOR. So she fluttered away, laughing, and disappeared among the trees, as well-camouflaged by her grime and tatters as were the fidgeting squirrels by their grey fur and rapid movement. Even the reverberation of her laughter through her five or six black teeth was closely akin to the tiny cursing of the squirrels: and I wondered who she was. But even more I was wondering what the devil it was I had bought from her. Surely I could never have been so foolish as to imagine there could really be a complacent greasy concubine stuffed up in this very ordinary kitbag which she had dumped here at my feet? It had the British Army broad-arrow stencilled on it in black and what seemed to be a soldier's number – 22128480. I tried to lift it up, it was heavy enough, certainly. But whatever was inside it was pure deadweight and had neither the shape nor the consistency of living flesh, female, lecherous idiots for the use of. So I gave it a kick. Hurt my foot. Then I tried to unfasten the string. But the rain had soaked it and all I succeeded in doing was to nearly break off a finger-nail. I was about to have a go at it with my penknife and my teeth when I heard footsteps behind me . . .

Heavy footsteps on leaf-strewn grass.

He had boots on his feet and they crunched the dead leaves, I looked up at him under my armpit, good God, how tall he was, he was hanging right above me the way colliery winding gear would overhang the little streets of West Yorkshire where I was born...

PARK-KEEPER. Oy. You.

NARRATOR. On his hat was a small brass badge: he was a park-keeper.

PARK-KEEPER. I said you. What's in that bag, then?

NARRATOR. I don't know.

PARK-KEEPER. Well, get it out of here. It's a Thing.

NARRATOR. Yes.

PARK-KEEPER. It's an Article.

NARRATOR. I suppose so.

PARK-KEEPER. It's an Object of Merchandise. You can't bring it in this park. You are a Vendor.

NARRATOR. No, I'm not.

PARK-KEEPER. And if you aren't, you are a Gipsy or Vagrant: or you are about to use the park for a Purpose of Immorality: and in any case you are in a condition such as is Offensive to Other Members of the Public.

NARRATOR. I most certainly am not. And what other members of the public? There's nobody else here.

PARK-KEEPER. That may well be *your* opinion. If you refuse to comply with the printed and posted regulations of the Greater London Council, I fear I shall have no alternative but to take your Name and Address.

NARRATOR. Yes, but –

PARK-KEEPER. Here is my notebook. Here is my pencil. Right then, we are prepared.

NARRATOR. His pencil was enormous, stuck weapon-wise in his belt, it was the kind that carpenters use, over an inch broad and a third of an inch thick, almost a cubit in length; and his fingers tightened on the shaft of it till the knucklebones sprang white beneath the skin. His book was the size of my grandfather's Family Bible, loaded to the endpapers with the names and addresses of all those who were accursed for that they lived in fornication, for that they were covetous and bore false witness, for that they moved their neighbour's landmark, for that they –

PARK-KEEPER. Go on, get out of it, and take your dunnage with you!

NARRATOR. He had lifted up the great stave that he carried under his swollen elbow, it was a pikestaff shod with steel, you could have murdered a bull with it, though for him it was but an implement for the removal of waste paper from the immaculate greensward. Like the steering oar of the 'Argo' he did poise it in the air, and so drove it with all his malice into the frayed canvas of my sack.

A squeal like an injured pig.

Oh – don't do that, you cause distress . . .

PARK-KEEPER. Get out of it.

NARRATOR. So I went. He followed me to the gate. I looked round after I had gone out of the park and there he was standing, his cruel spike still uplifted in his hand like a sword of living flame, protecting the fenced garden, and the squirrels, and the birds, and the rabbits, and the prohibited fruit of the glade, from the nonsense that was in my bag. So the question arose: what nonsense? I had heard it squeal when it was poked: but not the squeal of a woman. I was well aware by now that in that respect I had been deceived. At all events this bag must hold something that was known to be obnoxious to the guardians of the public amenity. So I thought it would be better not to attempt again to open it until I was well out of sight of nosey-parkers, bureaucrats, and my fellow-men in general.

Wind and rain noises continue, together with many bird-calls.

So I heaved it on my shoulder and looked carefully to left

and right in due dread of the passing traffic. But where was the passing traffic? Where indeed was the Muswell Hill Road, which should have run beside the park to the bus-stop and the road-junction and the Northern Line Underground? No road, no cars, no houses? All I could see was a wide heathery brackeny bushy sort of moor with clumps of dark trees here and there, and a trackway across it, a trackway which disappeared towards the south round the shoulder of a wet green hill – Highgate Hill? It might have been Mount Zion for as much as *I* could recognize. Beyond the hill, and several miles away, I could see a cloud of smoke, I supposed hanging over some small inhabited community. It was still raining: and it was cold. Bewildered by these circumstances, and resentful at the weather, I began to walk. South, towards the smoke. Before I did anything else, I must find out where I was. *When* I was. Who else there was, and why.

>This dream of mine
>That I had thought so fine
>Was now becoming burdensome and made
>Me mutter curses underneath my breath.
>It occurred to me it was no dream, but Death.
>If it was Death, why was I not afraid?
>Just mildly curious I was:
>And cross.

A muffled sound of women's voices wailing and croaking, as though from a little distance.

Then I realized that the strange noise that came out of an overgrown hollow towards my left was not being made by birds. I went down between the bushes.

Noise increases.

Here there was a group of women kneeling and crouching

round a man who lay on the grass. He was a long man in a black suit full of holes and covered with clay. He was dead.

FIRST WOMAN (*these women have harsh rasping voices like crows*). He was starved.

SECOND WOMAN. What else with but bad nettles to boil up for his soup?

THIRD WOMAN. Chewing roots.

FOURTH WOMAN. Cramming grass between his teeth till his mouth-water runs all green and his stomach swells out till it was ready to burst.

FIRST WOMAN. And it's burst.

NARRATOR. Who was he?

FIRST WOMAN. How should we know?

SECOND WOMAN. We just found him.

THIRD WOMAN. If we had strength enough, we would dig him his grave.

NARRATOR.
>The man upon the ground was dead.
>Bent down around him every head
>Seemed more than half as dead as his.
>I saw their black and yellow eyes
>Like rat-holes in a river-bank
>Where deep inside the rats will wink
>And blink and grind their savage teeth.
>Four savage women ground their teeth,
>Splintered tent-pegs or such cogs
>As millwrights cut from jagged logs
>They crunched together: then they swung
>Their necks towards me, stared at me long,
>In silence stared and then began
>At once and suddenly to scream and sing:

WOMEN (*in a kind of rhythmic dirge*).
>There he has it
>There he has food in his bag
>Tear it down from him

> Tear it and grab it and drag
> Rip off his fingers
> By root and by sinew
> Castrate him and rape him and beat
> For what he has got we can eat
> Eat eat eat eat eat eat . . .

Their chant becomes a terrifying mob-yell.

NARRATOR (*pleading futilely through their shouts and violent attack*). No no, stop it, God, ladies, give over, no, please – but I didn't even know who you were – I haven't got any food – here, you leave that alone – HELP – oh my God, HELP ME – they've gone mad –!

A growing thunder of horsehoofs and male shouting. The rage of the women turns to screams of fear.

> Indeed I had made quite sure that I was already a dead man. The four of them were swarming upon me like four hundred furious bees let loose from an upturned hive. Then suddenly they were gone and the ground all around where they had flung me was bouncing in my ears with the din of great horsehoofs . . .

A silence broken by occasional distant screams and shouts. The horsehoofs recede with these. Then one horse is heard returning. A jingle of harness as the rider reins up.

RIDER. Are you right, boy? Left alive, are you? By Christ, but we came just in time.

NARRATOR. He was a soldier of some sort, well mounted and heavily-accoutred in leather strapwork and brass-buckles, big boots, a thick black club in his hand, six or seven inch-wide moustache across his face, face all but entirely concealed under the wide peak of a black leather helmet. He had half-a-dozen men with him, all equipped in the same style. As I rose to my feet, very vague, very battered, I could see them riding down the hill away from us, waving their truncheons, scattering the tattered women.

> They uttered their blows without remorse
> By heavy stick and hoof of horse.
> Upon one woman's womb they trampled
> She lay in the gorse all bloody and crumpled.
> But I was alive
> And I would thrive.

I am alive. Yes, I think so. I thank you. Good God but what a business. Who were they?

RIDER. They were starving. Didn't they tell you? They have nothing better to do but rake the countryside for food and so near are they to death they care not a scratch for the death of any creature who will come between them and the sustainment of their bellies. This dead fellow on the ground here, had you not interrupted them, they would have eaten him blood and bone.

NARRATOR. But why is this happening? Has there been some disaster? Is there famine in the land?

RIDER. Those who deserve to eat, eat. So what about you? What do *you* deserve? Where are you from?

NARRATOR. I – er – I came from – from over there...

RIDER. You seem well-fed, decent class of a man, quiet and unlikely to give trouble to the honest and self-respecting populace. Do you intend to travel far?

NARRATOR. To be frank, I do not know. I don't altogether know anything at all...

RIDER. And that is as it should be. A confession of ignorance is more than half-way towards a fulfilled education. With fulfilled education you take a fit place in responsible society. But it's no part of my duty to let you travel around here on your own. As you've seen, it's far from safe. So put up your bag upon the back of my saddle – take a good grasp of my left stirrup – and when the patrol has reassembled, we will escort you into town.

He bellows to his men.

> Come along then, let's be having you! You've got 'em all upon the run there, no point in bothering further. You can form yourselves up again upon me, in column of route, and then we can proceed . . .

Sound of the horses trotting.

NARRATOR.
> The road we travelled was not good,
> Rocky and rutted, clogged with mud,
> The land on either side was bare
> With roofless cottages here and there.
> No travellers did we pass or meet,
> Though once I saw the prints of feet,
> Bare feet, in the mud, as though
> Some ragged man who had to go
> Unshod upon this road had seen
> My escort and had fled between
> The thorny bushes out of sight –
> No doubt he crouched there in his fright
> Until we were gone by. And then
> Where three roads met we came upon
> A leafless tree. To the trunk was nailed
> A living man who screamed and railed:

MAN NAILED TO TREE. For the freedom of the people, for the freedom of the people, for the freedom of the people – oh the starving men will live and the well-fed men will rot among the maggots of their own engendering . . .

He stops shouting and whimpers.

> For God's sake somebody give me a spoonful of water . . .

RIDER. No no, we ride past him, he's nothing, he don't signify: he'll be dead before tomorrow.

NARRATOR. But who *is* he?

RIDER. Like I told you: he's just nothing ... Take a look down the road ahead as we cross over this bluff: you'll get your first clear prospect of the town. So what do you think of it? Well-inhabited: and moreover well-protected: and it's my job to keep it so.

NARRATOR.
>There was the town and it was made
>Of wood and thatch. A tall stockade.
>Of sharpened timber rose around
>The huddled houses, and the ground
>Outside of this defence was scraped
>And scooped into a ditch. The moat
>Was dry, there was a drawbridge and a gate.
>The leader of my escort gave a shout:

RIDER. Ho-ho, ho-ho, ho-ho, ho-ho!

NARRATOR.
>The gate swung up, the bridge came down,
>We rode across into the town
>Beside the gate a sentry sprawled
>Loose in the lap of a fat brown girl.
>He wore a flower in his ear,
>He did not seem to take much care
>Upon his duty. In the air
>Above him flapped a worn-out flag
>Of tawdry stripes and patches, rather a rag,
>The whole town could be said to be
>Rather a rag. So slovenly
>Uncared-for were the walls and streets ...

To the rider. As voices and street-noises become heard.

>And yet the people whom one meets
>Among these slovenly uncared-for streets
>Are fat and greasy, richly-dressed,
>Hung with jewels, their curls well-pressed,

> Their necks and buttocks thick. Why then
> Is all their town untidy and unclean?

RIDER. When everybody is as rich as they are, who is left to do the dirty work?

NARRATOR. You are, are you not?

RIDER. Oh no, we are not. We keep the peace, preserve good order, we have clean clothes and polished gear, our breath don't stink. But then we're different, don't you see?

> We are of the town yet not of it
> In a well-swept corner there we sit –

NARRATOR. He pointed to a sort of compound on a hillock at one extremity of the stockade, fenced off very precisely in isolation from the rest: and there all indeed was neat and trimmed and whitewashed, with living quarters for both men and horses, a smart guard upon the gate, and nothing slovenly at all.

RIDER.

> We are without the town yet not outside:
> Day and night we march and ride,
> Ranging the high ground and the low.
> Where all is desolate we keep it so.
> These people live their scruffy lives because of us:
> We don't converse, we make no fuss.
> They only know that we are here:
> And, knowing that, they know no fear.

SECOND RIDER. Except of us.

THIRD RIDER. Except of us.

FIRST RIDER.

> Except of us. We make no fuss.
> We are quite content with what we do.
> Now, here, I think, is a fit place for *you*.

NARRATOR. And with a sudden twist of his foot he kicked me sprawling through an archway into a large courtyard that opened off the street. He threw my bag after me and then clattered away with his men.

Noise of horses receding. Now is heard the hum of a large crowd and music.

It appeared to be a place of assembly, with benches of rough-hewn timber arranged in tiers upon three sides, while on the fourth side, opposite the entrance, stood a raised platform under the shelter of a long sheet of tarpaulin stretched upon poles. The benches were crowded with people eating and drinking and sweating in the warm sunshine. The rain was over and I had begun to feel very hot. The smell in this courtyard was not at all agreeable and there was a good deal of pushing and shoving. I had hard work to keep hold of my bag, and I had more than a notion that many of those around me were thieves. Upon the platform a pair of dancers were performing for their entertainment. One dancer was a woman – she tinkled little cymbals as she danced, and her long draperies swirled all over the platform. Her partner was a wild-looking bearded man. He wore no more than a red-embroidered breech-clout and a short leather waistcoat. In his hands were two sharp knives with which he cut and tore at the draperies of the woman until she danced entirely naked. The people cheered and cheered at this progressive revelation. For myself, despite my earlier libidinous hopes in regard to the sack, I was more concerned in preventing my feet from being trodden on and my pockets from being picked than I was with the indecent excitement of the exhibition upon the stage. Then I became aware that the two dancers – now prancing arm-in-arm like a pair of yoked chariot-horses – had suddenly broken into song.

Cheers from the crowd as described: then silence for the song, which is accompanied by the cymbals and the stamping of the dancers' feet.

DANCERS (*singing*).

> 'Pharaoh lived in Egypt
> He dreamed a dream one night
> Seven cows were feeding,
> They were full and fat.
>
> Pharaoh lived in Egypt
> He dreamed another dream
> Seven cows came walking,
> They were long and lean.
>
> The lean cows ate the fat cows up,
> Pharaoh rolled around:
> Pharaoh hid his head then
> Deep in the ground.
>
> 'Joseph Joseph,
> Tell to me my dream.
> If you cannot tell it
> I must groan and scream.'
>
> 'Joseph Joseph –
> What does it mean?'
> Joseph said to Pharaoh:
> 'You are dead and gone.'

POPULAR MINISTER (*shouting amid the cheers and applause after the song*). Eat, drink, and be merry: for tomorrow you die!

More cheers and laughter.

NARRATOR. The dancers had moved aside, their place on the platform was now taken by a grey-haired smiling red-cheeked soft-handed dignified benevolent gentleman. He wore a robe like an academic doctor and a chain-of-office round his neck. The people loved him...
Who is he?

A VOICE IN THE CROWD. Sh-ssh, he is the King's Chief Minister.
NARRATOR. He seems a very popular minister.
VOICES FROM THE CROWD. The people love him ... He provides the entertainment, you see, from his own private fortune ... Just listen to the reception he gets.
NARRATOR. I can hear it. And he enjoys it.

A prolonged ovation for the MINISTER *is now under way.*

A VOICE FROM THE CROWD. Oh he does, yes.
NARRATOR. How did he acquire his own private fortune?
VOICE FROM THE CROWD. How do you think? He inherited it: like everybody else.
NARRATOR. Ah ...
But now the minister was making a speech ...

The MINISTER'S *voice is heard in broken fragments against a background of almost continual cheers.*

POPULAR MINISTER. Sugar and spice and all things nice ... It's a beautiful afternoon, look the sun's come out at last!
NARRATOR. From the way he went on you would think he had brought it out himself ...
POPULAR MINISTER. Delightful young lady ... give her a bit of a slap and tickle ...

Giggles and shrill female laughter.

NARRATOR. This was the female dancer, undulating on the stage there, within two or three inches of the Minister's gesticulating fingers: so he gives a poke to her cheeky plumpness and then more than a poke, he does not spare himself in his indulgence.

A brisk handclap

Then he claps his fat hands and two little girls with big round eyes and many bangles on their wrists came tripping on with baskets. The baskets contained what appeared to be sweets, wrapped up in silver paper, and he tossed them in handfuls to the crowd, and the crowd scrambled.

General excited shouts and scufflings.

Just for toffees – such a scramble?

VOICE FROM THE CROWD. Only some of them are toffees, some of them are pearls and emeralds . . . and some of them are dried beans . . . it's very much a lucky dip.

NARRATOR. Being a stranger I thought it best not to join in the scrambling myself. But the man on my left was unwrapping a real pearl . . .

MAN'S VOICE FROM CROWD. God be praised, God be praised, look at that, sir, there is richness!

NARRATOR. While the woman on my right was unlucky and got no more than a couple of the dried beans.

WOMAN'S VOICE FROM CROWD. Oh the devil, I say to hell with that. God, they were thrown to me on purpose!

NARRATOR. While the scramble was taking place the Minister had gone and the dancers had gone and the little girls had gone too. The platform was now empty.

Boos and jeers from the crowd.

Oh but no, it was not. Here's a tall stooping meagre-featured mean-eyed black-haired hobbling clothes-prop of a spoilsport and he walks with the aid of a stick. He snarls from the platform as the enraged people snarl at him . . .
Who is he?

VOICE FROM THE CROWD. Ssh-sh, he's the King's Chief Minister.

NARRATOR. But we've just had the King's Chief Minister . . .

VOICE FROM THE CROWD. No no, this is the Other Minister, who is not popular with the people. They always have to have the two of them – stands to reason, when you look at it . . .

UNPOPULAR MINISTER. Oh yes, you may boo and you may

cat-call, and you may make mock of my disabilities: but you know I know the real reason for your pretended scorn! Because I am the one, the only one in all this town to have the courage and the self-respect to inform you of the truth about yourselves, of the perils that do confront you, and of the faults of character through which you will be presently submerged by those same perils, if you do not look sharp about you and pull yourselves together – oh, you improvident dross and floating motes of sad debauchment! Yes, I tell to you the truth: and as truth it is not comfortable: and as teller of it I am hated. Well, do you want it, or do you not? Are you going to let me speak?

The outcry increases for a moment, then dies away.

Thank you. Now listen to this: the horsemen on patrol this afternoon have brought a stranger into town. I don't like the sound of him: and I don't like his looks. If you all turn around, you will see him at the back there – there he is – and if you are half the men I take you for, you won't like him either!

NARRATOR.
    It is not at all agreeable.
    To be glared at by all the people.
    I do not hold that man to be wise
    Who desires to be made the cynosure of all eyes.

UNPOPULAR MINISTER. You see, there he stands and his face turns from red to white and from white back to red again. Oh yes, while you were all soaking up the voluptuous depravity so generously provided you by the munificence of my esteemed colleague, you failed to notice, did you not, that someone had crept in, that someone's eyes were popping out at the sight of the private nudities that had been supplied for you alone, that someone at the back there was irregularly experiencing a carnal enjoyment of what was yours and yours alone: and he asked you no permission!

A threatening murmur from the crowd.

Come forward, sir, come forward, and make yourself known to this hospitable assembly. If you have a joke at the back we would all be glad to share it —

NARRATOR. The apologetic smile I was nervously assuming disappeared at once.

UNPOPULAR MINISTER. Or if you have a problem to be solved perhaps we all can solve it for you. Make a gangway for the gentleman; let him set himself up upon the platform. Up beside me, sir, if you please. Now, sir: face the people.

NARRATOR. So I faced them. By God I had no choice: they thrust me up there so violently that I twisted my ankle. And they giggled at me: giggled and whispered. One or two of them threw tomatoes.

Noises from the crowd appropriate to the description.

UNPOPULAR MINISTER. That's enough now, that's enough. Save your applause till the gentleman has performed. You will perform, sir, won't you, you will not disappoint us?

NARRATOR. But I —

UNPOPULAR MINISTER. What's your name?

NARRATOR. John.

UNPOPULAR MINISTER. He says his name is John. Do we think his name is John?

GENERAL SHOUT. No.

UNPOPULAR MINISTER. Oh dear, they don't believe you. So I wonder what your name is. He wears spectacles, does the little gentleman, he must be a gentleman of learning. Do you know what I think he is, I think he is a Professor.

NARRATOR. No, I'm not, I —

UNPOPULAR MINISTER. And just look at his little fingers — he has inkstains on his fingers! Professor Inkspot is his name and a very good name for him too. Shall we sing our little song to him? One: two: three —

CROWD (*sings, led by the* MINISTER).
>Professor Inkspot tell us now
>Why you walk like a pregnant sow
>Why your nose does root and dig
>Into the earth like a grunting pig
>Tell us tell us tell us quick
>Or else he'll whack you with his stick –

UNPOPULAR MINISTER. Or else I'll whack you with my stick! There!

Blow of cane and a cry, repeated.

>There again! Ha: so that's a foretaste. Now explain yourself and smartly. What have you got in that bag? More pens have you got, more bottles of ink?

NARRATOR. I do not know why I should be treated with such disdain.
>From my childhood ever I had felt great fear
>Of a crowd of strange men who would stare at me and jeer:
>But now when confronted by just such a mob
>For a moment indeed of all speech they did me rob:
>But then my sudden courage came out at them in pride–
>I would not be intimidated and my heart I would not hide.

My heart I will not hide from you, nor yet what is in my sack. I am not to be put to shame: and all that I have I am ready to declare.

UNPOPULAR MINISTER. Very well then: what is it?

NARRATOR. Except that I don't know: which is feeble enough, I will agree with you.

UNPOPULAR MINISTER. So open it up for us.

NARRATOR. I can't untie the cord.

UNPOPULAR MINISTER. Feeble-fingered idiot – use this.

NARRATOR. And he handed me a jack-knife and I cut open the bag.

THE BAGMAN

UNPOPULAR MINISTER. Hold it up from the bottom and shake out whatever's in it.

Sound of bag being shaken and objects tumbling out.

NARRATOR. Little men.

UNPOPULAR MINISTER. Little men? You're a little man yourself. So here is a little man with a bag full of little men. How many little men? Will you tell the people, tell them loudly.

NARRATOR. One, two, three –

little men and little women, the largest of them about twelve inches long, made out of wood and carefully jointed and carved. Each one of them dressed in a characteristic costume –

seven, eight, nine – there was a Soldier in a red coat, and a Policeman, and a Doctor with great spectacles, and a pretty little blonde Popsy and a blowsy soot-stained Housewife with a baby at her breast, and a hideous Old Woman, and a Robber with a great sword and bushy whiskers –

thirteen, fourteen, fifteen, sixteen – no, I counted him already – sixteen, seventeen, eighteen –

here were a King and a Queen and a Bishop with a hooked nose –

eighteen, did I say? I must have miscounted, I'll go back again to number twelve –

the funny thing was I couldn't count them at all, my whole notion of numbers seemed to have got muddled-up, so I came to a sort of compromise ...

I can't count them exactly, it's the sunshine, it's too dazzling, but I suppose it would be fair to say there are something between twenty and thirty of them. Attractive little people, don't you think?

I was still nervous of that stick.

UNPOPULAR MINISTER. But what are they for?

NARRATOR. Ah, yes, what are they for ...?

I stood upon the platform with the bright sun bang in my eyes, I had a headache, oh God, in this confined courtyard what a stink of overfed and belching bodies – and for what seemed many minutes I stood there in complete silence. A little flurry of wind had set the tarpaulin to rattle and to strain at its cords, and everyone in the crowded place was suddenly as still as death. When I spoke I did not speak with my own voice, nor did it seem to me that I myself had composed the words that I uttered: but it was as though curled up inside my belly a very old and cantankerous dragon was growling and orating: and the sound came through my teeth:

In a strange distorted voice.

> My little people in a row
> Sit on the stage and watch the show.
> The show they watch is rows and rows
> Of people watching them. Who knows
> Which is more alive than which?
> If you fidget, if you twitch,
> Blow your nose or nod your head,
> My little men, though made of wood,
> Can frame a gesture just as good.
> Laugh and leap or shake with terror,
> My little men will be your mirror.
> What you do or what you did
> From little people can't be hid:
> They will know it and reflect
> In strut and jerk your every act –
> Your thoughts expressed in dark of night
> They body forth in broad daylight.
> This Soldier-boy in coat of red
> Is every one of you whose head
> Is turned by dreams of power achieved
> Through violence and the tears of the bereaved:
> This Constable so stiff and straight

Is any man who thinks that Right
Must stamp on Wrong till Wrong can claim
That Right was twice as much to blame:
And see this bright-eyed Girl, her bum
Round as an apple or a plum.
She is any girl who will lie down
Whether for love or half-a-crown,
And rising up again, will say:
'That's enough then for today,
Do not expect as much tomorrow.'
This Mother here, in joy and sorrow
Becomes the mother of you all –
Her Baby from her lap will crawl
And grow to be whichever one
Of you you would he should become.
Who is to say what stories these shall shew you?
You tell me who you are and I will know you:
And then you sit and watch my little men
And you will know yourselves again again again
Again again again again . . .

In his normal voice again.

And no sooner were the words out of my mouth (good heavens, but I had reminded myself of Adolf Hitler at his worst, and what were people going to think of me? Even these appalling people!) – no sooner were they out of my mouth than all the little men had leapt to their feet, and there upon the platform, without a moment's pause or hesitation they had formed themselves up into two opponent groups. There was a small group of those in rich costumes, and a large group made up of the ragged and ill-favoured. Straightway the larger party flung themselves with rage upon the smaller: But were beaten back time and again by the valour of the Soldier and the brutality of the Constable – there was also some display of the duplicity of the Bishop and the cruel faint-heartedness of the King and Queen: but in the end the larger party were compelled to fall to their knees, abase themselves, and sue for mercy. Then the revengeful King decreed various punishments: the leaders of the rebellion were killed in hideous fashion, or flogged and tormented, or locked up in iron cages without food and water. Their cries so worked upon the spirit of their defeated comrades that a new conspiracy was set afoot, the King was assassinated, the Bishop was beaten, the Soldier and the Constable were put to flight, and their overweening Queen was dragged tumultuously through the mire. Such prisoners from the former rebellion as still survived their ill-treatment were released and paraded as heroes, and in fine a Republic was proclaimed and the victors of the civil war rejoiced in their great deliverance. Yet all their efforts in the end were seen to be in vain. No sooner had they prevailed upon their sumptuous enemies than they fell to quarrelling amongst themselves as to which of them should hold the sovereignty. The conclusion was ominous. Hacked and splintered wooden limbs lay everywhere upon the platform, and of those manikins who were not dead only the most crippled and the weakest seemed to have enough voice to bewail their illfortune and to call upon the world for redress. None who watched were able to restrain their tears. The more so because all this time an unseen music had been ringing and clanging, stirring the heart and turning the entrails of all that spellbound auditory –

So it has and now it ceases.

– and when at last it fell silent and my little people reassembled themselves, rose once again to their feet, and lifted their right arms in a gesture of courteous dismissal – there came a roar of spontaneous applause that shook the very boards on which we stood.

Applause, as described.

Even the unpopular minister was smiling – in a thin and grudgeful fashion, mind you: but smiling he certainly was.

UNPOPULAR MINISTER. Most impressive. Educational. I am truly amazed, Professor, that upon so short an acquaintance with our community you have been able to diagnose our weaknesses and discover our public perils with such acute perception. How much more salutary than the pabulum served up through the munificence of my esteemed colleague.

POPULAR MINISTER (*voice in crescendo as though he is quickly approaching*). Your esteemed colleague, my dear sir, is entirely of the same opinion as yourself. Professor, I congratulate you. I have never known the people so delighted, so enlivened, so thoroughly stimulated both intellectually and emotionally as they have been this afternoon. Indeed, I think that you and I should have a little talk about some further demonstrations of the same kind, which I trust I may prevail upon you to perform for us very shortly. You will stay with us for some time, of course, we can offer you the very best facilities for the exposition of your strange powers: no expense need be spared. In the meantime –

As crowd starts clapping in slow time.

UNPOPULAR MINISTER. In the meantime, dear colleague, the people are getting impatient. There is business-of-state to be attended to in this Assembly, now that the entertainment is over. Brigands from the outside who were captured by yesterday's patrol have to be brought to trial, sentenced and punished: and there are numerous new regulations for the Security of the City that require to be debated and approved before His Majesty can issue them in form of a Decree.

POPULAR MINISTER. But all this can be dealt with by Junior Members of the Council. The professor here and his

innovation must surely be discussed by you and me, forthwith.
UNPOPULAR MINISTER. Whatever you wish...

He addresses the crowd.

Rabble: be silent! You have not been forgotten. Indeed you are never forgotten.
POPULAR MINISTER (*addressing the crowd*).

In the midst of jeers and cheers.

The Junior Magistrates will attend to the next business, if my colleague and I may have your courteous permission to leave you in their charge...

Baying and booing.

Thank you... Thank you very much... Professor, will you come this way?
NARRATOR. As they led me from the platform, the meeting was called to order...

The noise of the crowd recedes. A magistrate is heard appealing for silence.

MAGISTRATE. Citizens, if you please, I call this Assembly to order –
NARRATOR. – by a red-faced loud-voiced Serjeant-Major type of man who had risen from his seat in the front row and was greeted by a shower of orange-peel and apple-cores and nutshells, for his pains. I had gathered my little men into the bag and I followed the two Ministers down a corridor into an ante-chamber.

A door slams, shutting out most of the noise of the crowd.

Here they left me to my own devices with a bottle of wine and a plate of ginger biscuits. I sat there for say ten minutes. I could hear their voices in the next room. I am sure I was not intended to hear, but some holes for ventilation had been left unstoppered up near the ceiling, and their words of necessity came filtering through...

The MINISTERS' *conversation is heard very indistinctly at first, then by degrees more clearly.*

UNPOPULAR MINISTER. No no no, you are altogether too indulgent. Oh he has these powers, certainly, and considerable skill in their deployment. The question is: how much is him, and how much is his little men? Is it sorcery or conjuring: does he mean to do it or does it happen? We'll not find how to deal with him until we know the answer to that.

POPULAR MINISTER. I do not regard the answer to that as being at all important. Whether it is magical or whether it is calculated, it is perfectly clear to me that the whole performance was informed by the fellow's own personality. So we must act, must we not, as though he intended it all from the very beginning?

UNPOPULAR MINISTER. Very well, let us do so. And precisely *what* did he intend? Subversive encouragement to insurrection and revolution. Setting up the cause of the outlandish men against the citizens. And quite amazingly, the citizens, or the great part of them, applauded.

POPULAR MINISTER. It was exciting, as a narrative, you must grant it that; it had fast movement, confrontation, violent excess of sympathy swinging rapidly to and fro –

UNPOPULAR MINISTER. Sympathy. The audience felt sympathy. Sympathy for the mimic spectacle of their own appalling overthrow. What kind of people *are* they?

POPULAR MINISTER. Very much like any other kind. They know themselves fat because the outlandish men are thin: they suffer now and then in their consciences for this. Either we can help them to forget it, as I do: or else, like this Professor fellow, we can occasionally remind them, let them feel a temporary pang, and their discomfort is assuaged.

Surely this has always been *your* technique. What's wrong with it so suddenly?

UNPOPULAR MINISTER.
>It is altogether one thing to make them afraid
>At rebellion and destruction.
>Quite another to have them urged in open daylight to feel glad
>That such violence can already be conceivably in contemplation.
>Put into their hand a knife with a sharp blade,
>Tell them 'this is for your heart,
>Would you rather have it in your throat,
>Do not forget to offer praise before you die
>For the skill of the knife-grinder
>And the truth of his hand and eye'?
>I ask you: is that politic?
>I tell you, no, it makes me sick.

POPULAR MINISTER. Not altogether as stupid as you would make me out to be. The story concluded after all with the complete failure of the rebellion to consolidate its achievement.

UNPOPULAR MINISTER. I did not consider it a logical development of the plot. And if I did not think so there are likely to be others who would share my opinion.

POPULAR MINISTER. But the fact is they are well-fed and they do not want to be otherwise. Look out of the window, my dear sir, and tell me what is going on.

NARRATOR. I had no window in my room but I could hear sounds from the outside...

Screams and cruel laughter, rather faintly heard.

UNPOPULAR MINISTER. Yes. The brigands have been tried and are being put to death in the name of His Majesty. The Assembly is appreciating the act of justice. And so?

POPULAR MINISTER. And so they are appreciating it and their

enjoyment of the execution is in no way diminished by their enjoyment of the recent spectacle, however subversive you may think it has been. In my view the Professor is a young man to be encouraged: though of course we must be careful.

UNPOPULAR MINISTER. Oh, whatever you think best. We can encourage him by all means. And control him.

POPULAR MINISTER. Not control. Suggest directions: that is all...

Their voices fade away.

NARRATOR. You will think me very stupid, but the significance of this conversation entirely passed me by. I was so tired, you see, I could hardly keep open my eyes. All I could think of was the power and the splendour of my little men, so newly revealed to me, so manifold in possibility, so outrageously out of proportion to the amount of actual work I had done – they had been absolutely given to me, from where I knew not, and by whom I knew not. But it appeared that they were mine: and I alone was capable of inspiring them into their motions . . . After a little the two ministers returned, they spoke to me in soothing voices, they promised me this, that, and the other –

MINISTERS' VOICES (*through* NARRATOR'*s speech*).

Peace and quiet . . . agreeable surroundings . . . appreciative audiences . . . plenty of opportunity for experiment . . . unlimited funds at your disposal . . . and as for any small personal gratifications appropriate to your status amongst us . . . only say the word, my dear fellow, you have only to say the word . . .

NARRATOR. But I think I had already fallen asleep. There was some sensation of being led or carried through one room and then another, and of being laid upon a bed. At any rate there was a bed and I was on it: and I slept.

    Yet even asleep I still did keep
    The cord that tied my precious bag

>   Tight in my grasp, lest one should drag
>   It from me secretly by night.
>   Mistrustful I was. I was quite right...

YOUNG WOMAN (*in a whisper*). What is this cord you grip so tight?

NARRATOR. This cord...?

YOUNG WOMAN.
>   You clench with all your might
>   Your little fist. I cannot prise
>   It open. Like a dead man's eyes.

NARRATOR. Hey-up – ho ho – so I've caught you, have I?

YOUNG WOMAN. Let go of my arm, you are hurting me – please!

NARRATOR. No no, you first tell me what you are doing here. Putting out your hand in the dark to grab hold upon my bag: but you grabbed hold upon *me*: and I've got you: so explain yourself and no nonsense.

YOUNG WOMAN. Perfectly happy to explain myself, sir: but keep your voice down. There may be other people awake besides us, late though it is. I came in here as instructed by the Ministers of the King: I am what they call a small personal gratification appropriate to your status – you will have seen me already – I was dancing upon the platform.

NARRATOR. Oh, you were?

YOUNG WOMAN. Yes, I was.

NARRATOR. A most depraved performance.

YOUNG WOMAN. Yes, it was.

NARRATOR. And why should the ministers imagine that I would enjoy your company any further at close quarters?

YOUNG WOMAN. I don't see why you shouldn't – everyone else does.

NARRATOR. Very possibly. But none the less, you had your hand upon my sack.

YOUNG WOMAN. Oh yes, sir, that also was according to instructions.

NARRATOR. Then you'd better get out and be damned to you before I kick you up the –
YOUNG WOMAN. Oh come on, you are half-asleep still. How the devil would you have known I had my hand upon your sack unless I had whispered in your ear that I had, so woke you up?
NARRATOR. And that's a good point . . . Have we not got a light in here – I'd like to have a look at you.
YOUNG WOMAN. We are striking no lights, there are no shutters to the window. What I was told to do I should have done in the dark, if they see a light they will be suspicious. But move over into the moonlight. Now then . . . can you see me?
NARRATOR.
> She was not beautiful; but her eyes were big.
> Protuberant. They shone like the white of an egg.
> The hand by which she held me was wide, hot and strong,
> Her lips were thick, her nose was long.
> We were quite alone in a narrow plastered room.

Is there anyone listening outside the door?
YOUNG WOMAN. There might be . . . Have a look?

Footsteps on a wooden floor, door opens and shuts.

NARRATOR. Nobody there.
YOUNG WOMAN. Good. Now I am going to tell you what they would kill me for if they heard of it. It will not have escaped your attention that the people of this town live a comfortable life.
NARRATOR. True. And as I take it, you yourself are part of that comfort.
YOUNG WOMAN. Nor yet that the people outside are dying of starvation?
NARRATOR. That's true too. And no one could deny that you have a belly on you like a tub of butter.
YOUNG WOMAN. But you don't know why?

NARRATOR. No.
YOUNG WOMAN.
>So here is the secret:
>Make sure that you keep it.
>By right I should compel you to swear a great oath
>To the burning of your flesh and the shedding of your blood:
>But I do not: so take note –
>It is not possible I should be anything but stark raving mad.
>So being mad, I will begin.
>In the very middle of this town
>Is a deep dark hole struck into the ground,
>Kept well-guarded and closed-in
>By a roof of slate and a wall of stone.
>Day and night selected men
>Descend by ropes to dig and shovel:
>And what they find there as they grovel
>Far underneath us in the dark
>Keeps us as jovial as Midas when
>He touched the door-frame of his but-and-ben
>And turned each rotten timber post
>To what it was he wanted most.
>There is a cave of clay there choked
>With jewels deep in the core of the rock –
>Emeralds, rubies, brooches of gold,
>Every turn of the spade down there will unfold
>A crown or a coronet, a great plate or a goblet
>Or maybe just two or three pearls in a droplet
>Or a thick twist of silver wire for a necklet or armlet.

NARRATOR. And how did it all get there?
YOUNG WOMAN.
>How do you think? It was left there
>By rich men who were frightened, and ran
>From some conqueror or other, in the ancient times.

> We are told that these rich men had committed crimes,
> Murdered and pillaged – for what other reason
> Would they have gathered so much in so short a season?
> We call this dirty town the Town of the Murderer's treasure
> And we live on it and live off it,
> And we make of it our pleasure.

NARRATOR. So nobody has to do any work.

YOUNG WOMAN. None of the citizens have to do any work.

NARRATOR. And the outlandish men, to whom you deny any share of your riches?

YOUNG WOMAN. If they work for us, we feed them. But we don't need very much work.

NARRATOR. Who are they?

YOUNG WOMAN.
> Who do you think? You are too slow
> To understand what you ought to know.
> They are the original murderers who dug the hole and buried
> All that we dig up and all that we inherit.
> The citizens came in
> One bright year in the season of spring:
> They took everything they found
> Above and below the ground:
> They dwell in a town which they did not build
> And they give the name of murderers to the men whom they killed.

NARRATOR. Is it citizens – *they*? A minute ago you said *we*. Who are *you*?

YOUNG WOMAN.
> I am betwixt and between
> Neither the one nor the other
> My father was outlandish
> He crept in and took theft of my mother

And after that he went back to his old trade as a highway
   robber:
An hereditary enemy of the town where his daughter
   was born.
They let me live and I can feed and survive without
   harm
But I must deserve my protection
By obeying their every instruction
And whatever they do to me
I must have it done to me with charm.

NARRATOR. You are a slave.

YOUNG WOMAN. No more than they are. Because the treasure that they think is theirs isn't theirs at all. There is a great King across the water who takes as much of it as he wants, provides the citizens with the food that ought to be being grown upon the farms of the outlandish men – if they had farms, which they once had – he determines his own price for the treasure that is dug up, he has an ambassador in this town to supervise the diggings, and he appoints and pays and administers the horsemen who ride patrol – the ones who brought you into town. Oh, the whole economy of this region is entirely ridiculous – you wouldn't credit it if you met it in real life: but then you are in a dream, and you have entirely abdicated, have you not, from the regiment of common-sense?

NARRATOR. I don't know about dreams – I dreamt I had a young woman in my bag to make love to me, but it wasn't so. Would you be inclined to make love to me now? I would like it, if you would?

YOUNG WOMAN. No, take away your fingers from where you are putting them or I will bite them off this minute – it's not that kind of dream at all. You have fallen asleep at the wrong place and the wrong time: and besides I was instructed to make love to you and I have suddenly turned today into a mood of rebellion. You know why?

NARRATOR. Why?

YOUNG WOMAN. Because of your little men and the wild memory they dredged up of who my father once was and the strong defiance with which he lived. You send us more remembrances like that, little man, there will be no protection left, no security, no good dinners, nothing but the truth.

Footsteps quickly on the floor, door opens and shuts.

NARRATOR. And at once I was alone in the room without any sign that she had been with me, except for the rancid smell of her breath in the air – such bad breath they all had in this place. For people who lived so voluptuously but in what I now knew to be imminent peril they were extremely indelicate over the detail of their common intercourse. I wished I was back in Muswell Hill – the whole situation was becoming most unpleasant.

> When I fell asleep I had thought my dream would be
> The gulf-weed slowly stroking me on back and side
> The dream of a jellyfish in a warm and waveless sea
> No turbulence to contradict the gentle ebbing of the tide:
> I was quite wrong.
> I was not strong.
> I did not think I could survive this kind of sleep.
> I staggered up and down, piercing my feet
> Upon the splinters in the rough-cut floor.

His nervous footsteps.

> I flung open the door –

Sound of door opened.

> Looked out into a passage-way
> And there was no one there.
> I said to myself: I will escape

>   I will run barefoot upon splinters and stones and thorns
>   By dint of the pain of it I will surely awake.
>   This town and its cruel people
>   Are made only of a vapour
>   Of falsehood and dirt –
>   I will awake from them and work
>   As is my custom without confusion
>   Upon a clean piece of white paper.
>   In a clean quiet house with the windows closed
>   And flowers upon the window-sills elegantly disposed
>   And my wife between my white sheets
>   And my children in the green garden
>   Four children and one sweet wife
>   Every one of them with the name of Arden.
>   Let me run, let me run quickly –
>   Oh God, how the soles of my feet have been torn!

OFFICIAL. Forgive me, but you go no further. I have orders to bring you and your bag directly to a person who is wanting to speak to you.

NARRATOR. Oh . . . I haven't got any shoes on. Let me go back to the room for my shoes.

OFFICIAL. Oh no, that is not possible. Had you been sleeping peacefully I would have woken you with circumspection and let you dress yourself at leisure: but as it is I have run into you in the grey light of dawn apparently in process of making your escape. You are a guest of this city, sir, it is discourteous of you to attempt to evade us: therefore you must come with me, and at once, just as you are. Where is the young woman who was sent to your room to sleep with you?

NARRATOR. I – I sent her away. I did not want her. She was not attractive.

OFFICIAL. You are the first I have heard say so. Come with me, please . . .

NARRATOR. He carried a black wand with a silver knob – some

THE BAGMAN

sort of a tipstaff, no doubt: but there were two men behind him with clubs, so I could not refuse his invitation. I did put one nervous question –
Where? To whom? Why?

OFFICIAL. You must not put questions to His Majesty's Servants.

Footsteps as they go.

NARRATOR. So – ho – it was the King they were taking me to, was it? But they led me through no glorious forecourts and tall porticoes of a palace. Down one back-corridor, across a dingy yard, up another corridor, duck through a storeroom amongst barrels and boxes, and so at length into a vestibule about the size of a large tea-chest and here we all four stopped. There was a four-foot-high door in the whitewashed wall opposite us, and the tipstaff knocked cautiously, opened it, stuck his head in –

Knock on the door, opening door –

OFFICIAL. Just to check that they're all ready for you. Yes, they are – in you go.

NARRATOR. And he pushed me in and went out himself and the door was shut behind me.

Door shuts.

AMBASSADOR. Sit down, there's a stool in the corner.

NARRATOR. A great big man with a face like a bucket of blood. He sat behind a table in a room surprisingly clean, painted and gilded, with life-size pictures of soldiers on every panel of the walls. Each soldier held a different sort of weapon the blade of every weapon had dark-brown stains upon it, the faces of the soldiers were like wild animals, with tusks. The sunrise was coming in through little windows high up near the ceiling. The great big man was eating eggs. He ate seven eggs at once and the yolk ran down his chin.

AMBASSADOR. Now then, what's all this, then?

NARRATOR. Your Majesty, I –

AMBASSADOR. Don't call me majesty. Only one majesty in this town, boy, and he's too small.

SECRETARY. You are in the presence, young gentleman, of the Ambassador of the Great King across the water.

NARRATOR. A bespectacled secretary with his face covered with cobwebs, he crouched in the dark behind the door, stabbing flies with his pen-knife. I had not noticed him when I came in.

SECRETARY. You will address the Ambassador as Excellence: because he is.

AMBASSADOR. So you hear who I am.

NARRATOR. Yes, I do – Excellence.

AMBASSADOR. Quiet. I am the enormous Ambassador. I eat eggs and they make me fat. What do you do? Don't tell me. I've been told. You set afoot unauthorized imitations of people you should despise and you blow them out like bullfrogs with the imagination of their strength. *At* the same time, however, you reserve to yourself a sharp pin with which you can at your own convenience prick their distended bellies and explode them into nothing. The first part of your programme, from my point of view, is abhorrent. From the point of view of the underdog people to whom you address yourself, the second part is likewise. Therefore you are very bold, and a man to be objectively admired: or else you are a hedger and a fencesitter, and a contemptible poltroon. I wonder which? In any case you are a man who deserves to be suppressed. But I am not going to suppress you. No: nor am I going to encourage you. I am going to regard you as a challenge and defy you to do your worst. In some sense it may be said that a challenge to us, in this place, is both desirable and requisite . . .

(*In an undertone.*) . . . at least a challenge that we are aware of – for it will attract to its publicity the other, occult, challenges of which at present we have no cognizance, only suspicion . . .

SECRETARY (*likewise in an undertone*). Rather more than suspicion in several cases, Excellence. I am compiling – as you told me – all these dossiers, and there will be certain surprises in the fullness of time –

AMBASSADOR. I don't want to hear them now . . . Boy, you sit there hostile, upon my stool: are you dumbfounded or are you goddamned stubborn? Yes, he's stubborn: yes, he's bold: by God we do admire him. Yes, we lack such men round here. You're going to shake me by the hand!

NARRATOR. His hand had an egg in it. He thought it was funny.

AMBASSADOR *roars with laughter*.

Raw yolk splashed up my sleeve and dribbled between my fingers. Then he threw another egg at the Secretary.

More laughter.

Hit him square upon the spectacles, streaked with white and yellow all the cobwebs across his face.

A strange gravelly noise.

At first I didn't know what the noise was: then I realized it was the Secretary laughing, because the Ambassador was laughing . . . But now I heard this other noise I was not able to account for. Oh God, but it was *me* laughing . . . I suppose I thought it was appropriate and I didn't want to give offence. Never willingly give offence, not me – a disposition always, so I thought, to be both meek and courteous. The next damned egg that the arrogant bastard threw landed right in the middle of my chest.

AMBASSADOR (*still laughing*).
>Eggs are full of gold
>They stink when they are old.
>Scramble boil or poach or fry –

> Long and hard oh you may try
> You'll never scrape away the stain –
> The egg is mine and you are mine.
> Go on. Get out. Good-bye . . .

NARRATOR. The Secretary got up, with a sudden and novel politeness he threw open the door for me – not the small back door by which I had entered: but the proper and painted door of state at the other side of the room, he ushered me out, all deference, into a gallery full of male and female dragon-flies – or so it seemed, so elegant they were, gracefully waving their adorned bodies in this and that inconsequential gesture, one towards the other, and they chewed at little sweetmeats, took discreet sips of little drinks out of thimble-sized crystalware, and buzzed, and then fell silent, and smiled and winked at me as I passed through.

Buzz of conversation, tinkling laughter.

I saw among them the two ministers whom I had seen the previous day but no one else that I recognized. The two ministers were very gracious – smiling at me: but they said nothing. Everyone was looking at my bare feet and my untidy appearance – when all was said this was the audience-chamber of the palace of the King and I was dressed for nothing better than the *Evening Standard* in Muswell Hill – yet there was no malice, there was no scorn, there was a kind of respect about their looks. Just so, I could hear them thinking, comes arrayed the man who holds within his bag the lovely secrets of our lives – so intimate his burden, so abrupt and unmannerly his looks – they found the contrast quite delicious. Then there was a –

Sennet or tucket or fanfare.

– a trumpet, out of Shakespeare, as it were, and the King came in and the Queen, and various other members of the Royal Family, I don't know who they were. Everyone knelt down, except for me – I was a Republican, I said to myself, and I would go on my knees for no man. But I felt a certain embarrassment after standing alone for a long minute, and I began to bend my knees like everybody else, but half-heartedly, in order to show my disapproval of these forms. But the King spoke:

KING. I see you do not kneel.

NARRATOR. I straighten up again, quickly. If he had not noticed my beginning to bend then I might as well appear to be consistent in my disapproval.

No, sir: I do not. I am a Republican, you see.

KING. Yes, you would be. I suppose we all are, these days, are we not? Though you would get a dusty reception in the palace of my cousin, the *Great* King, over the water. But he is a barbarian, really . . . er, his Ambassador's not come in yet?

UNPOPULAR MINISTER. No, Your Majesty, not yet.

KING. Thank goodness for that . . . Very well then, young man – er – Professor, are you called? You may open your bag again and begin. We are yours to command.

NARRATOR. Then they all sat down, put their hands upon their laps, and looked expectantly at me. Somebody clapped –

A small applause, checked by indignant whispers.

– but was immediately shushed. I bowed to them, smiled, opened up the bag, took out the little men, and laid them down upon the polished floorboards in a row, just as before. And just as before the cantankerous dragon inside me began to give tongue . . .

In his distorted voice again.

> My little people in a row
> Sit on the stage and watch the show.
> The show they watch is rows and rows
> Of people watching them . . .

But I felt less at ease than on the previous occasion. I had reminded myself then of Adolf Hitler – Hitler in his prime, at a Nuremburg rally, perhaps – now, if I was Hitler, it was Hitler in the Berlin bunker of 1945, and the boots of the Red Army were stamping above my head. But I got through it and I got on with it and the little people began their story. Not at all the same story. I was amazed at their metamorphosis. They were not even the same sort of people as before. There was a King and a Queen and a Bishop, yes, but the Soldier and the Constable and the Housewife and the ragged men were all gone, their places had been taken by a crowd of posturing exquisites, dolled-up in peacock feathers and waterfalls of gold and silver lace. And there was no fighting in the story. Nothing but extraordinary variations of erotic postures and intrigues, couplings and triplings and quadruplings, men and women together, men and men, women and women, women and men and women – while the audience muttered and laughed and clapped a little and conversed one with another. Some of them walked out. The music was erotic also, but more than a little insipid. At the end, when all the diverse and perverse setting-to-partners had been, in a manner, resolved, there was a courteous but unenthusiastic applause –

Music ends, some clapping etc.

– and I felt ashamed. First because I had not liked the entire narrative from beginning to end, and second, because the audience had not liked it very much either. Or so at least I believed: but when half an hour afterwards I found myself closeted as an honoured guest, in a small and private room with no other than the King and Queen, I began to wonder if I had not been mistaken.

Music playing – a lute.

The King was no more slender than the general run of his subjects: but he was gentle and timorous and kind-hearted.

The Queen was soft and dewy: you could almost call her silly – if she had not been wearing a crown.

KING. So very glad to have this opportunity of speaking to you, my dear Professor.

QUEEN. So different from what we thought you would have been.

KING. But the exhibition itself, the little men – I mean –

QUEEN. Not at all what we expected.

NARRATOR. Oh . . . what did you expect – er – Your Majesty . . .?

KING. Something much more – much more –

QUEEN. Much more flattering, His Majesty means.

KING. We never speak to anybody except flatterers and – and panderers. It was quite a relief to hear the – hear the truth about ourselves.

QUEEN. Yes, it made us squirm.

KING. Indeed, yes . . .

NARRATOR. I did not know whether or not I was expected to say anything . . . Yes, I – er – I try to do my best – Your Majesty . . .

QUEEN. So you do – yes . . .

KING. Yes . . . Tomorrow – at the same time?

NARRATOR. The audience being over, I was shewn to the breakfast room where I ate a huge meal. And the next day at the same time I went through the same performance, and the next day, and the next day, and for days upon days, so it seemed, though there was a kind of odd telescopic effect about the progress of time, and in some way I was not certain but that only a few hours had passed. When I was not employed in demonstrating my powers before the assembled royalty and courtiers, I was left to enjoy myself in the gardens of the palace (for so it was called by everyone, for all that it was no more than a collection of well-decorated summer-houses, cleaner than the town outside but in no sense monumental). Yet gardens it did have, and they were furnished with silver fountains, and marble tables laden with food and drink, and plenty of sumptuous girls reclining in their jewels who didn't have anything interesting to say, but permitted me all manner of familiarity whenever I wanted it. It was all very indolent and agreeable, and very much beside the point –

The lute music has become accompanied by the faraway singing of a renaissance madrigal, the patter of water from a fountain, the voices of birds, and the laughter of women. Suddenly this is broken into by the voice of the YOUNG WOMAN, *hard and direct. The music etc., stops abruptly.*

YOUNG WOMAN. And that is a true word. Not only beside the point – you are entirely beside yourself. Wake up.

NARRATOR. I *am* awake – you are always waking me – it is no business of yours and in any case I don't believe you have permission to be in the King's private garden.

YOUNG WOMAN. Private garden?
    Turn your sleepy head from left to right
    Tell me what you find here in your sight.

NARRATOR.
    I turn my head from left to right, right round –
    I find myself – on a gravelly patch of ground
    Strewn with cinders and old rags,
    Rusty buckets, broken jugs.
    Where is the fountain, where is the green grass,
    Where are the girls whom I dreamed that I did kiss?
    Where is the King who spoke to me so kindly?
    Can this be his bright palace, all this rubbish piled around me?

YOUNG WOMAN.
    Within your dream you fell asleep again.

NARRATOR.
    But when did I fall asleep, when did it go wrong –?

YOUNG WOMAN.
    Look at your shirt, boy, look at the yellow stain.

NARRATOR. The egg of the Ambassador – was that the first or second dream?

YOUNG WOMAN. That was the true dream: now I'll show you the true King –

NARRATOR. And stooping through brambles and bits of broken wall and old fences made of useless bedsteads, she brought me secretly by back ways to a derelict shed like a henhouse – you see many such if you go to Dagenham or Romford on the top deck of a London bus, hundreds of them scattered all over the allotments, sordid enough but useful for the men who grow cabbages when not working in the factories. But there was no cabbage-patch here, and the window of the shed was nailed up with creosoted boards. We looked in through a chink between these and it was all dark inside the shed –

A rustling of straw, chink of a chain.

A FEEBLE OLD MAN'S VOICE (*same speaker as the* KING). For the liberty of the people, for the liberty of the people, oh God is there nobody who will give me a drink of water ...

NARRATOR. Who is it, who have they got in there – is he chained to the wall, or what?

YOUNG WOMAN. Chained to the wall, and has been for twenty years. When they remember, they give him something to eat and drink. That is the King, and this is all that is left of his palace. Now we'd best get out of here before we are caught by the guard.

Heavy footsteps drawing nearer.

S sst – it's too late, get down among the nettles –

Rustling of undergrowth. Footsteps halt.

GUARD. Stay where you are – who goes! Come out of that and declare yourselves!

YOUNG WOMAN. No no, not yet, not time to declare ourselves yet – put your hand out to the left, what do you find?

NARRATOR. There's an iron ring fixed into a flagstone.
GUARD. I said come out of that – I can see you – all right, then, you want it the hard way –

He blows a whistle and shouts.

Get the dogs, there's two intruders –

More shouts and whistles from a distance. Running feet. The angry yelp of guard-dogs.

YOUNG WOMAN. Pull at it, you fool – it'll come up if you pull strongly, oh for God's sake, look sharp with it!
NARRATOR. It's difficult, the clay all round seems to have set hard – ooh – ugh – aah – I've got it open!
YOUNG WOMAN. Down into it – quick. What the devil are you playing at!
NARRATOR. My bag, I can't leave my bag –
YOUNG WOMAN. God, you'll *have* to leave your bag – you idiot – you –
NARRATOR. No. Aha, I have it. Here we are –

Slam of trapdoor closing, noise of guards instantly shut off.

YOUNG WOMAN. – safe and sound. There's bolts underneath the trap. Shut them.
NARRATOR. Damned rusty . . .

Bolts being dragged.

Do they know about this place? Did they see where we went under?
YOUNG WOMAN. I don't think so – they would have seen us go in among the bushes, and with the dogs they'll soon find the trap. So it can't ever be used again. There was a project, never got anywhere, to rescue the old King this way. Now of course it's finished. But it wasn't any good, the old King's no good to anyone, the fact of the matter is there is nobody any good to anyone, nobody and nothing – except to burn the whole town down. We'll have to do it one of these days –

easy enough, all made of wood: but for some reason nobody wanted to – afraid, I wouldn't wonder, though they *said* they were too humane.

NARRATOR. Where are we?

YOUNG WOMAN. We're in a disused drainpipe. All the old drains in this town are disused. You could tell that from the smell, when you walk about the streets.

NARRATOR. Can we get out anywhere?

YOUNG WOMAN. Not conveniently. It used to lead to the river, but it has been blocked up with dead dogs and so on, there are other trapdoors, we'll find a good one and climb up that way, but we'd better wait till after nightfall. And would you leave that bloody bag behind you – you're going to get stuck in the passageways or goodness knows what – as it is you've already nearly got both of us caught with it!

NARRATOR. I can't leave it. Whatever would I do without it?

YOUNG WOMAN. Just the same as the rest of us – fight.

NARRATOR. Fight . . . but I didn't come here to fight – I was given this bag – to – to – look, I *paid* for this bag: gave all the money I had in my pocket – don't you see that it is all that I have?

YOUNG WOMAN. Which is more than any of the rest of us have. *We* don't need it: *you* don't – get rid of it.

NARRATOR. And who do you think you are talking about – the *rest* of you? – it's the first time I heard –

YOUNG WOMAN. It's the first time you could possibly have heard it – the first time I have ever said it – the first time it has ever happened. This is not just a matter now of little gangs of bold marauders (God rest my father's soul, but that was all that he was) no, it is even *unity*, controlled and organized resistance – we are solidly put together, we are under discipline and we look for power – by God for the first time for how many hundreds of years it is power we are going to get – we are going to get it, in our own hands!

Sudden cheering: cries of 'for the liberty of the people' from many throats, echoing as though in a confined vault.

NARRATOR. And there they all were, crowded in a close dark underground cavern – their emaciated faces lit by flaring torchlight, their fists clenched towards the roof in fantastic ecstasy, their purposeful bodies hung with weapons of every size and variety, from flint axes and bows-and-arrows to great rusty blunderbuss-guns. My young woman, my lascivious dancer, she who had been instructed both to spy upon me and seduce me, now dragged me by force forward into the middle of them all and – without consulting me – proclaimed me to be their brother.

YOUNG WOMAN. He is our brother!

Cheers.

NARRATOR. No; you don't know that at all. And if indeed you are preparing an insurrection in this catacomb, may I tell you that your sense of security leaves a great deal to be desired? As far as you are concerned I'm a complete stranger, yet you bring me into the midst of you and reveal to me your plans. You must be mad.

YOUNG WOMAN. Not at all.

NARRATOR. I could betray you.

YOUNG WOMAN. Not at all. For you are asleep: this is your dream. How can you betray what you have done no more than dream about?

NARRATOR. Oh, very well then, provided that that is clearly understood by all parties.

>So: in my dream, I ask of you
>To tell me what I am to do.
>Outlandish men, who rise in anger
>Against the tyrant and oppressor:
>What do you want from the lonely stranger –
>Beyond that I should share your danger

> In, of course, so far as I can?
> Lumbered, as I am,
> With this most discommodious
> But necessary burden –

Generally scornful laughter.

A MAN'S VOICE.
> Your burden is no good to us
> Throw it down – take up a weapon –

NARRATOR.
> This *is* my weapon!
> You have your spears and knives:
> I have these images of your proud lives.
> Here in your secret hold, your dangerous den
> I straightway dedicate to you my little men.

So I tore open the sack and tipped them out in front of the company. I was exalted, my heart burned with zeal – I was not a fighter, I was no conspirator, I had no power but this power and I was giving it all to the cause. There was nothing of Hitler in my voice this time – Savonarola perhaps, or Oliver Cromwell on the dreich moorland of Dunbar –

> My little people in a row
> Sit on the stage and watch the show –

Strange crying voices like birds in a box.

LITTLE MEN. No no, no no, no no, no no –
NARRATOR. I looked down at them in amazement, they were all clustering and huddling together, some of them struggling to get back into the bag – they had the appearance of a whole colony of ants distressed beyond their wits when a violent boot breaks into their anthill – What are you doing – why do you not respond to me – you have your business to perform – for God's sake get on with it – would you put me to shame before all these men of war?

LITTLE MEN (*one very high thin voice dominant*).
>   Men of war do not require
>   To see themselves in a truthful mirror
>   All that they need to spur them to action
>   Is their own most bloody reflection
>   In the white eyeballs of their foe.
>   We are neat and well-considered little people –
>   If you bring us into battle
>   You bring us only unto grief and woe
>   Fracture and breakage that we cannot repair
>   They will snap our wooden joints
>   And pull out our cotton hair.
>   Please let us please let us get back into the sack
>   When the battle has been won
>   We can peep out again and creep back.

A SUDDEN MAN'S VOICE (*as though running towards them underground*). Comrades, stand to your weapons, we are betrayed, the enemy is upon us – they have got into the tunnels –

YOUNG WOMAN. We are betrayed by this fool with his bag – he has wasted our time and distracted our attention – I warned him, I warned him, he must not bring it here –!

NARRATOR. And in an instant all was blood and death and furious weapons swung at random in the dark.

Great noise of fighting.

> The young woman who had brought me there was struck down at the first onslaught – I endeavoured to get between her and the soldier who was beating her to the ground but he thrust me aside with a great backhand blow – I fell down upon my sack and upon the squirming heap of my terrified little men – a huge foot, shod with steel, stamped hard upon my temple. And that was the end of my dream.
>   I awoke upon the platform
>   Of the Highgate Underground Station –

> A train was just departing
> The passengers thronged in and out
> The porter at back of the crowd
> Gave his customary shout –

Noises of underground station – 'Mind the doors please' etc ...

> I staggered a forsworn traitor,
> To the foot of the escalator,
> I mounted the moving stair
> Came out into the upper air.
> In my hand I held a bag
> It was a kitbag from the Army,
> I looked in it – it was quite empty.
> I dropped it in a litter-box
> And walked home sideways
> Like a slinking fox.
> At the corner of Muswell Hill
> By the National Provincial Bank
> Stood an ancient gipsy beggar-woman
> With black hair long and lank.

She spoke to me in an undertone – I make no doubt she was only asking for the price of a bunch of white heather, but the roar of the traffic distorted her voice and all I heard was what she could not possibly have uttered.

OLD WOMAN (*among confused street noises*).

> You did not find what you expected
> What you found you did not use
> What you saw you did not look at
> When you looked at it you would not choose!

NARRATOR.

> So I pushed past her and went home.
> If I had been defeated it was all in a dream.
> But the fat men and the thin men
> Stood all around me in the street –
> I could not carry a fat man's body

Upon a thin man's feet.
It would have been easy it would have been good
To have carried a bag full of solid food
And fed the thin men till they were
As fat as the men who held them in fear
But such is not the nature of these bags
That are given away by old women in rags.
Such is not my nature, nor will be.
All I can do is to look at what I see . . .